D1520830

3/15
3×1P

9/14

If You Are the Son of God

If You Are the Son of God

The Suffering and Temptations of Jesus

JACQUES ELLUL

Translated by
ANNE-MARIE ANDREASSON-HOGG

Foreword by
DAVID W. GILL

CASCADE *Books* · Eugene, Oregon

IF YOU ARE THE SON OF GOD
The Suffering and Temptations of Jesus

Cascade Books
An Imprint of Wipf and Stock Publishers
199 W. 8th Ave., Suite 3
Eugene, OR 97401

www.wipfandstock.com

Translated from the French Si tu es le fils de Dieu: souffrances et tentations de Jésus (Paris: Centurion, 1991) by Anne-Marie Andreasson-Hogg.

Si tu le fils de Dieu, le defi et le nouveau.
© Éditions de la Table Ronde, 2007.

ISBN 13: 978-1-62564-258-5

Cataloging-in-Publication data:

Ellul, Jacques, 1912–1994

　　If you are the son of God : the suffering and temptations of Jesus / Jacques Ellul.

　　viii + 96 p. ; 21.5 cm. —Includes bibliographical references.

　　ISBN 13: 978-1-62564-258-5

　　1. Jesus Christ—Temptation. 2. Jesus Christ—Passion. I. Title.

BT355 E45 2014

Manufactured in the U.S.A.

Contents

Foreword

If You Are the Son of God: The Sufferings and Temptations of Jesus is a remarkable little book by Jacques Ellul (1912—1994). Known to most of the world for his massive sociological studies of the character and impact of technology on modern life, Ellul was also throughout his life a passionate follower of Jesus with a long and steady flow of published writings as evidence.

If You Are the Son of God is in the style of his earlier thematic studies of Meaning of the City and Money and Power in that it tracks a topic through the text of the Bible, making interesting and often surprising observations along the way. Ellul argues that our translations of the Apostles Creed misplace the punctuation. We should say "He suffered" (period); then "Under Pontius Pilate he was crucified." Thus, suffering characterized his whole sojourn on earth, not just the end. Certainly the life of Jesus was not suffering alone but Ellul helps us see how completely Jesus participated in the wounded, broken condition of humanity. He was fully human with no supernatural exemption from our pain and suffering, be that physical, relational, spiritual, political, or any other. He was certainly the "Suffering Servant" of Messianic expectation.

And in Part Two Ellul shows how Jesus was also tempted and tested in every way faced by man and woman. Fully human, with no superhero protection built into him, Jesus was tempted and tested in all ways: economically, politically, religiously, even sexually and psychologically. Ellul's meditations on the Three

Temptations at the outset of Jesus' public ministry will challenge and stimulate all readers.

Ellul's suggestion that suffering and temptation are closely related is thoroughly demonstrated in this little book. His unpacking of the roots of temptation in our humanity and circumstances and refusal to see "Satan" and the "Devil" as merely external, personalized, cosmic figures will certainly illuminate—but may also frustrate some readers. As always, Ellul is full of bold ideas and assertions, brilliant and original flashes of insight, and debatable conclusions. But this is vintage Ellul in that we encounter a free, creative, thoughtful, learned, passionate, and controversial wrestling with the biblical foundations of the faith. While you will not learn any of this from his text, it should be pointed out that Jacques Ellul himself suffered the privations of the economic depression of the Thirties, the repression of the Nazi Occupation and the horrors of war, the death of a son in childhood, the illness of his beloved wife, and his own marginalization as an unconventional thinker in both academy and church.

No one leaves Ellul without being challenged to their roots but at the same time helped to better understand and more fully appreciate the Bible and its central figure.

David W. Gill
November 2012
President, International Jacques Ellul Society
Mockler-Phillips Professor of Workplace Theology & Ethics
Gordon-Conwell Theological Seminary
South Hamilton, Massachusetts

INTRODUCTION

The Suffering and Temptations of Jesus

"True Man and True God"

Throughout this study, we will endeavor simply to read the Gospels attentively, without imagining anything and without losing anything. Insofar as we are reading them from the perspective of suffering and temptation, our focus will obviously be on the man Jesus, the son of the carpenter from Nazareth. We readily acknowledge that Jesus was fully man and fully God. However, we are all familiar with the temptation of favoring one or the other of these aspects. For centuries, we have seen in Jesus first of all the Incarnation of *God*. Being fully God meant that he did not really suffer exactly like us: his divine quality transcended his suffering. Furthermore, the suffering was sometimes regarded as being limited to the six hours of the crucifixion, as the change in the punctuation in the text of the Creed indicated. We often recite, "He suffered under Pontius Pilate" (so he only suffered under Pontius Pilate!) and then, "He was crucified." Yet, the actual text (which conforms to the Latin grammatical construction) reads, "He suffered; under Pontius Pilate he was crucified." From the life and teaching of Jesus, the authors of the Creed only retain one reality: he suffered. This is in complete accordance with the fact that he fulfilled the prophecy of the "Suffering Servant."

In the same way, we are often tempted to think that his crucifixion—during which he obviously was in pain—was not quite equivalent to that of the other two men who were crucified, for example, because . . . he was God. He must have been able to endure suffering more easily. And what of his death? As God, he knew that he would rise again, which made his death different from the deaths of all men!

Such ideas and such spontaneous feelings are absolutely not in keeping with an affirmation of the full humanity of Christ. When one reminds the faithful of this humanity in regard to less burning matters, one notices that they are often actually scandalized: "Did Jesus really share the errors in geography, in physics, in astronomy of the people of his time?"—"But since he was God . . . he knew everything." But since he was fully man, he did not know more than other men. He took upon himself the *whole* human condition, without any pretenses or copouts.

The question will burn even hotter when we look at the development of the phrase: "He was tempted in all things . . . ," that is, as an ordinary man in the Gospels. A film by Martin Scorsese, *The Last Temptation of Christ* (which is quite poor, if I may add!), caused a scandal because we cannot imagine that the temptations of Jesus were of all kinds and that they were genuine temptations. Involuntarily, we think, "But because he was God, it was easy for him to resist the temptation! He knew it was a temptation, so he could easily say no. But for us . . . !" The Gospels tell us that this idea is equally false.

As we will show more fully, it was the case that any temptation was suffering for him; and all suffering implied a temptation—and much more than for us! When we suffer, we cannot do anything about it (except make use of doctors and medication), whereas he, as God, could have ended the suffering. He could have chosen not to experience it, but in order to remain on the level of man, he did not make that choice. He let himself be led to the slaughter like a sheep. We will attempt to adhere to the Gospels, which perfectly show us the human, the fully human, condition of Jesus.

The Jesus of History and the Jesus of Faith

It is true that over the past decade or so theologians have changed sides. It used to be fashionable to distinguish between the Jesus of history and the Christ of faith. This is an elegant way of disposing of the problem. You may keep the Christ of faith, the Messiah, the Son of God, the miracle worker, the Risen One. None of this may be false as far as faith is concerned—it has in any case been invented by faith and for faith—but it cannot be retained by history, that is, it cannot actually be part of the life of Jesus because these facts cannot be ascertained by means of the historical method[1] and are implausible from the point of view of reason. For history can only observe reasonable facts, a necessary presupposition. As for the Christ of faith—who is certainly not to be rejected—in this view, he seems to have been an invention of Paul, who made use of the person of Jesus. We may therefore leave him to believers. Let us note that this is a very old theory made new by different vocabulary; it is the old theological theory of "liberalism-rationalism": anything in the Gospels that cannot be explained rationally must be rejected. History has now become the referee rather than rationality, but it amounts to the same thing. It separates the man from God, separates Jesus from the Christ.

We have a good example of this historicization in the novel *L'Ombre du Galiléen* by Gerd Thiessen.[2] In this novel, we see some laudable efforts to retain everything that can be retained without doing harm to rationality or historicity. This is the case, for instance, with the astonishing "explanation" given for the miracle of the feeding of the five thousand. We know that certain wealthy women helped Jesus: Jane "says" that she would send him bread, fruit, etc. Some such delivery must have taken place that day. The crowd considered the "appearance" of this food a miracle, and because it was now clear that no one would be lacking, each person then took out his own bag of provisions that he had earlier hidden.

1. Let us note that the other "facts" reported in the Gospels cannot be ascertained in that way either!

2. Thiessen, *L'Ombre du Galiléen.*

Thus, everyone was fed. The miracle was only the disappearance of everyone's selfishness! One can thus keep the story with just a little twist, exactly as the author *has* such or such a character in the novel *report* the story of the miracles (it is said among the people that . . .) or a certain teaching (it was told that . . .). So the novel preserves what is plausible in the *mouths* of simple men. But it is not at all real! Let us leave such clever fiction aside.

If we thus retain the Jesus of history by separating him from the Christ of faith, all the elements of suffering and temptation become normal, plausible, and even obvious. Provided that the Jesus of history is only a man like all others, it is obvious that he was tempted. After all, Scorsese's film is simply depicting what is normal and not scandalous at all. We have now gone to the other extreme: this Jesus of history suffered and was tempted, but there is absolutely no point in talking about it. This is why "natural" histories of Jesus almost never refer to the topic.

Later, we shall come back to another aspect of the humanity of Jesus that leaves aside his role as Messiah and Son of God. A few years ago, many theologians were focusing solely on the *political* Jesus. Of course, he was a politician of the left, a socialist, a revolutionary, a patriot fighting against the Romans, and so on . . . (As I have often remarked, the idea of Jesus the socialist is not at all new.[3]) So we find both theologians and historians who are in complete agreement as to his humanity, but retain only one aspect, the political one.

In its aspect of weakness on the one hand, and in its aspect of "moral problems" on the other, the humanity itself is completely set aside; these are not very interesting for the ardent politician or the ardent revolutionary. To retain the humanity of Jesus only to make him a combatant against the Romans or a freedom fighter or a gang leader or a skilled politician (some have spoken of the "revolutionary strategy" of Jesus, which destroys him historically, for his strategy was worthless—or at least was much poorer than that of Spartacus!!)—all that is to mock Jesus by forcing him into

3. See Barbusse, *Jesus*.

the ideology of the primacy of politics and the platitudes of Revolution! Such a "humanity" of Christ seems to me *trivial* and would not have warranted the faith, the commitment, and the preaching of those who followed him.

Listening to the Lament of Jesus

Thus, no matter where I may turn, I cannot find anyone who is striving to listen to the lament of Jesus about his suffering or the feeling of his weakness in the midst of temptation. Moreover, we must realize that if Jesus really is the Son of God, this perfectly human suffering is a temptation thrown at God Himself. It is certainly not curiosity that makes me read the Gospels again in this light but rather a desire to deepen my understanding of the relationship between the Father and the Son and thus my understanding of the Father. My purpose is not to move sensitive souls by writing these lines. This brings us to another serious aspect of my search.

When I speak of the suffering of Christ, I do not by any means intend to present "a theology of suffering." This is not about *participating in the suffering* of Christ. No, quite the contrary, it is about Jesus, the Christ, participating in our own suffering. Similarly, I do not intend to rewrite Søren Kierkegaard's *The Gospel of Suffering*. There are many beautiful things in that book, but it is nevertheless one of the rare works by Kierkegaard that I cannot fully embrace. I believe that the suffering of Jesus is in no way good news *to him*. For us, Jesus now comes infinitely closer—and by our suffering, we can share in his suffering! Let us by no means, however, go any further than that. Learning that Jesus suffered must not lead us *to want* to suffer.

Here again Jesus is exemplary: He never *sought out* suffering. Despite my reluctance to criticize mystics and others of that mold, I must say an absolute "No" to any seeking after suffering and instead affirm that what was traditionally called "the mortification of the flesh" is fundamentally anti-Christian. To portray a suffering Jesus is to say that he was like us. To be like him implies that we accept suffering when it comes, but certainly not that we want to suffer. I grant that such a desire is caused by a morbid orientation of Christian piety, obviously coupled with erroneous theology, a theology of the value of suffering for salvation and our redemption. A terrible double error is made here. Firstly, it is wrong to believe that the suffering of Christ "acquired" our salvation, when it is actually his death—by fulfilling all the sacrifices—that testifies to the love of God and to the grace that is given to us. Secondly, suffering would then be among the works that we perform to ensure our own salvation.

The belief that making oneself suffer can please God explains many indignant reactions on the part of non-Christians. They rightly ask, "Who is this Christian God who requires that his followers kill one another, whip themselves, cut themselves, and torture themselves, and who finds pleasure in this?" That is obviously the opposite of the God revealed by and in Jesus Christ. No, from the biblical point of view, suffering is a horror; it is an act of "Satan," the "devil's" pleasure. In this respect, the Book of Job gives us the *final* word. Nowhere in the book is suffering portrayed as a good thing or a positive value, rather it is a scandal in creation caused by the breach between humanity and God. Certainly, like Jesus, we are called to bear with suffering and temptation and remember the connection between the two, which we will see as we read the Gospels. And when we suffer, we should not say, "God is sending me this suffering, so I will bear it with joy." God does not cause anyone to suffer, and neither does he tempt anyone, as we shall see. Yet, we can live out our suffering in such a way that it carries us far from God (the evil God is making me suffer); or it can make us love God more by teaching us that God is present in a particular circumstance when he seems so far away! The gospel of suffering *may* be found in that understanding. Once more, however, I want to emphasize that we should not see any dolorism in this reading of the Gospels.

There remains one more question that agnostics often ask concerning this topic: "If God wants suffering, then any means to combat it—such as medicine—would be contrary to God's will." I have already given an answer to the erroneous presupposition of this kind of "reasoning." We must remember that, according to the Gospels, Jesus healed all the suffering with which he was confronted. There is often an *ad hominen* argument when I am asked this question: "Since you are against technology, you must be hostile to medicine!" I am in no way hostile to medicine or surgery. I fully accept medical work as long as it is not detrimental to an *aspect* of God's work. In any case, suffering is inexhaustible, as medicine is discovering today! Each time one kind of suffering is vanquished, another rears its head. This is also true of diseases! Now that tuberculosis, a horrible and devastating condition, has been overcome, cancer follows on its heels to take its place. It seems that we are on the eve of being able to cure cancer, and now, AIDS is spreading. Keep on healing, please keep on healing, for there will always be enough suffering around us and within us!

What applies to the struggle against suffering also applies to the struggle to end poverty, to end social injustice, or to search for a better distribution of wealth! How could I ever be "against" such causes? Because Jesus said, "Blessed are the poor . . ."? For almost two centuries now in France and in Europe as a whole, we have ceaselessly been seeking justice and an end to poverty. Yet, what I observe is an increase in another kind of suffering, for example, in communist countries. Economic poverty, which is actually increased in those countries, is not the only kind of poverty. Of course, we should fight poverty by all means possible! When Jesus proclaims to us that "You will *always* have the poor among you," he certainly does not mean "Leave things the way they are; do not do anything about it," but rather that "You will never exhaust the immensity of poverty and of all kinds of poverty."

It is important for us to meditate on the suffering of Jesus as the bearer of the total human condition—a quite humble and everyday suffering, anyone's suffering, and in the same way temptations comparable to the ones we encounter! This is the humanity of Jesus: a man—not a superman, a total man or a perfect man above the human condition—no, any little Jewish man with his joys and his sorrows. Therein lies the terrible scandal of the Incarnation:

God, all of God, came into this "Uomo qualunque," this "every-man," who, while bearing God, remained completely submissive to the human condition. My only claim is to attempt to show that, as one begins reading the Gospels and only the Gospels from this perspective on the suffering and the temptation of Jesus, one is astounded at the number of texts that mention this in passing, as it were, with a brief word.

What Does Temptation Mean?

Now, I must say a word about temptation. First of all, one needs to reaffirm very clearly that God does not tempt anyone. The text from the Epistle of James is adamant: "When tempted no one should say, 'God is tempting me.' For God cannot be tempted by evil, nor does he tempt anyone" (1:13). Even if we translate temptation by the word "trial," God does not take any pleasure in submitting his children to trials in order to see if their faith and their love would endure. At the very worst, God can, as we see in the prologue to Job, allow Satan to "tempt" a person by *challenging God*. Paul reinforces the certainty: "No temptation has seized you except what is *common to man*." So the well-known translation that reads "Lead us not into temptation" or "bring us not into temptation" is absurd.

Evil

Would temptation then be the work of an Evil Spirit? Possibly, as long as we do not personalize this spirit and as long as we do not make the Devil and Satan characters comparable to that of a person, even the spirit of a person! I have often said it: "Shatân" is "the Accuser." Wherever there is a (human) accuser, a spirit of accusation, there is Shatân—but people are sufficient for this to be the case. When one man accuses another, he is part of shatân (common noun!). The Shatân is only the composite, the synthesis, the sum total of all the accusations brought by people against other people in the world. There is no "spirit" independent of a person that would "inspire" him to bring this accusation. It wells up from man's heart all by itself.

In exactly the same way, the *diabolos* is the spirit of division. It is not that I want to dismiss the *exousiai* about which Paul is speaking when he says that we are not struggling against flesh and blood but against the rulers (*archa*), the authorities (*exousisai*), the princes of this world (*cosmocrates*), the spiritual forces of evil (*pneumatika tes ponerias*): here are the enemies that are "spiritual" and that may reign in high places . . . but this does not imply the personification of each one; rather it means that any *archante*, any authority on earth, whether it be political or of another kind, has its double, its twin, its corresponding entity, in a sort of "excess" that ensures its power and its domination in the world. It is the same for every *exousia*: the same word designates the earthly magistrate and this spiritual "celestial authority." In reality, it designates the reverse of any power. We can never meditate too much on the famous maxim that "Power corrupts, and absolute power corrupts absolutely."

We can say that there is never a good magistrate or a just authority! As soon as man has any power over others—whatever it may be—he is corrupted. This corruption does not manifest itself in torture, in an excess of power, in fraudulent financial dealings. . . . No, it is the simple, very direct domination that is corruption in itself. This corruption is so abstract, so minute, so subtle that political analysis cannot detect it; and it will take on a "spiritual" dimension and escape man's power and his virtue. This is why Paul says that it reigns "in high places." It is the "surplus"—of which I have spoken in other writings concerning money—that remains when we have analyzed all the other rational factors of political power. No matter how detailed it is, this analysis always comes up against the question: "Why does one obey, in general, and without rebelling against this authority?" There is the surplus of human corruption, of the one who commands, corresponding to the corruption of the one who is commanded—just as there is complicity between the propagandist and the person subjected to propaganda, as I have shown in other writings. It is undoubtedly the most subtle form of sin common to us all.

Thus, all temptation is human. God does not tempt us, and neither does any "devil" outside of us. The beginning of a solid analysis is presented by James (1:14): "Each one is tempted, when, by his own evil desire, he is dragged away and enticed." The key to temptation is the covetousness that is in each of us along with its other face, which is called the spirit of power. I would say that "covetousness" includes all the origins of temptation, but where it concerns human beings, it takes the form of a spirit of power. So once again, I will speak of covetousness because it is the key to our question; and James understands this perfectly! *Covetousness is the source of all sins.* There is the lust of the flesh, which is the most trivial and coarsest one, and the lust of the eyes (should it not include art?) and the lust of life (the pride of life, 1 John 2:15–16). In citing lust and pride, we are back to the spirit of power. Everything comes from this covetousness: it is from "inside" *the heart of humanity* that it all comes: thoughts of hate, adultery, murder, theft, greed, homosexuality, maliciousness, lies, lewdness, slander, pride, and, finally, folly. All of this comes from covetousness. Jesus himself said so (Mark 7:20–23).

All of this leans on two powerful buttresses: One is the *last* of the Ten Commandments: "You shall not covet anything." I say that if it is the last one, it is because it is the conclusion as well as the synthesis. You shall not covet the manufacturing of a god at your own disposal (second commandment). You shall not covet possession of the name of God. You shall not covet your neighbor's possessions (theft), your neighbor's wife (adultery), your neighbor's life . . . Everything is rooted in covetousness. The other buttress of this interpretation is simply the text in Genesis describing the breach between humanity and God, in which we find the *two* levels of covetousness: the woman looked at the tree and saw that its fruit was pleasing to the eye (lust of the eyes), valuable for opening up the mind (lust for knowledge . . . of what kind?), corresponding to the covetousness aroused by the serpent: "You will be like gods capable of determining what is good and evil." The absolute covetousness—to be like God!

Everything derives from this and especially from what we experience in our present world, that is, the proclamation of what is obviously evil as Good (for example, killing for one's country or for the party or for religion) and proclaiming as evil what God has called good (for example, challenging authorities, fighting for real freedom, for the true autonomy of a person . . .). This covetousness reaches its zenith when it is brought to bear on the Other. It is then the opposite of love. It is the domination of one over the other, whether the other is the woman, the child, the vanquished, or, formerly, the Black; and the spirit of power now inhabits Islam and sets it against the West.

Covetousness and the spirit of power have an individual character living in each one of us, yet because *all* have this inner covetousness, the whole social body exalts it. This produces the phenomenon of *exousia.* All the individuals comprising a social group produce not only an accumulation of power, but also a surplus, which gives society its boundless character as far as the individual is concerned and creates an ultimate meaning that constrains each individual and that makes only the group *seem* legitimate—hence the absurd interpretation of "democracy." A spirit of power to the second degree—and a covetousness to the second degree—will spring from this social group and will give us a feeling of absolute truth as well as an urge to satisfy our personal covetousness in the way opened up by this social group. So temptation finds its origin in our person and its justification in the social group that often makes its fulfillment possible.

Yet, for temptation to exist, it is not enough for covetousness to be present. It could remain locked in our heart and confine itself to tormenting us. James says that we are "enticed," dragged, lured. There must be some exterior circumstance—a meeting, an event, whether fortuitous or brought about intentionally—that activates covetousness. The man thirsting for money would not steal if there were not the sudden encounter with money at his disposal (or almost so . . . it would be so easy to get those millions that are within

reach). The man inhabited by Eros may remain tormented and re-
pressed until he meets the woman who abruptly becomes for him
the Woman and who seems to be welcoming him. Temptation is
thus the combination of covetousness and circumstance.

The encounter will not change anything if covetousness is not
present in the least. Covetousness will not be expressed if there is
no opportunity. All of this, as we can see, is perfectly simple and
natural. There is no need for a devil or a mysterious power. All of
this, James tells us, begets sin: "After desire has conceived, it gives
birth to sin." In order to see God's intervention in the meeting of
covetousness and circumstance, we would have to subscribe to the
non-biblical idea that God commands every miniscule event. No,
God has nothing to do with temptation either. Humanity and the
social group are quite sufficient.

Was Jesus Tempted?

We are now faced with a terrible question that we can only ask with
trembling: Was Jesus tempted? Really tempted? It is not enough
simply to quote the gospel text on the three temptations—a text
that we will later consider in detail. We will answer that Jesus the
man was tempted. Yet, he was also Jesus the Christ, the Son of
God, and God himself. Here is the great difficulty: if we say that *because* he was God, *he could not really* be tempted, we will fall back
into the previously-mentioned error in regard to suffering. This
pseudo-temptation would only be play-acting because, as God, he
could not yield to this temptation! This is very similar to the play-
acting resulting from certain theologies (they only pretended to
crucify Jesus, and so on). One thus turns the gravest, most solemn,
and most decisive adventure of all of humanity into a parody. No,
Jesus was indeed really tempted. We will see this throughout the
Gospels.

But we must not stop there: Why was Jesus tempted? Was
he tempted by the devil? Was he only tempted at the very beginning? Not at all! On the contrary, what is important is to see that

throughout his ministry, the same temptations are presented to him by various and multiple men and would address a potential covetousness in him.[4] I know that I am scandalizing some readers here: men are the ones who challenge the Son of God and God himself; men are the ones who actually tempt him precisely because he is the Son of God and God himself. I will even venture to say that the three temptations at the beginning were understood and written down by the gospel writers *ex post facto,* that is, as they understood which temptations Jesus was subjected to throughout his whole ministry, they summarized them in these three prefatory temptations. Here, the devil is only the representative of all of humanity and speaks in its name. He is only an artificial and symbolic character, the real tempter being humanity, both individual and social.

Has this not already been proclaimed in the revelation of the First Testament with humanity's challenge to God as embodied in the Tower of Babel? In the contempt for God in Gomorrah? In the anger of Jonah against the God who did not fulfill his own prophecy? The adherence to forms established for a relationship with God and about which God so often laments, "My people, what have I done to you that you treat me thus?" Yes, we are in truth now up against the wall! It is not God who tempts a person; it is the pseron who tempts God and provokes him to anger, vengeance, and extreme domination, which are possible for God. If God were to give free rein to these, he would cease to be the God of Love.

The actions of people are constantly tempting God the Father not to be the God of Love! This is clearly seen in the hard life that Jesus led. The Christ was tempted in all things. Owing to that, he suffered beyond any human suffering. This is because if he had wanted to, he could have cancelled this suffering and made the temptation void. He could have done that, but to secure the

---

4. Remember the famous text of Phil 2:6, in which Jesus would have considered equality with God something to be grasped. This has been remarkably taken up in the Koran: "If there had been another divine person (the Son), it is obvious that it would have wanted all of divinity for itself and would have dethroned the Father"!

salvation of all creation, it was necessary that he not do it.[5] Thus we do not only tempt ourselves and other people. It is God himself that we *put to the test*. After tempting God, we are finally subjected to the same temptation.

Light in Darkness

To conclude, I would like to emphasize that the relationship "suffering/temptation" is in its entirety contained in one sentence found at the beginning of the Gospel of John, a sentence that we sometimes read with a lack of thought: "The light came into the darkness, and the darkness did not receive it."[6] The darkness of beliefs and ideologies, the darkness of lies and religions, the darkness of the evil that a man does to himself, to his neighbor, to those far removed from him, the darkness of society over its members, the darkness of reason and of science . . . Our universe is made up of darkness; the more human knowledge advances, the more we understand this and the more the knowledge of the world advances, the more certain this becomes. The Light came. Not "one" light among others, as of course some lights might shine among people, but the light, "the light of all lights." This light *could* dispel all darkness. And it knew that it could. But the darkness would then have had to receive it. In order to be a real light, it could not conquer by force or overcome by force. It would then have ceased being light and would have started playing the game of darkness and would have become darkness. It glows and shines, but only within the limited circle that receives it. This light that came to enlighten the world suffers because it is not received, just as the risen and glorified Christ will not enter by force. "I stand at the door and knock" (Rev 3:20; *still* like a beggar). "And I, the mighty Lord, I am waiting for you to open the door for me." This is the temptation of the light,

5. Incongruously, I would like to mention one of the formulas employed for the coronation of the kings of France, a formula that has an obvious Christian inspiration: as the chancellor of the kingdom would say, "Sire, you can do all things, but you cannot want all that you can do."

6. This is the wording of the Segond translation of the Bible in French.

coming from the light to remove the darkness permanently. This is the suffering of the light, as it does not do this but chooses to overcome through love and without any constraints. Here is the summary of the life of Jesus. Here is where we encounter what is most profound in love. "Come, but I do not force you. I free you. And now, come."

PART ONE

The Suffering Servant

"SURELY HE TOOK UP our infirmities and carried our sorrows" (Isa 53:4). In other words, no human suffering was unknown to him. We should not neglect the simplest and most humble of these sufferings even as the texts invite us and allow us to see the more profound and essential suffering. Let us be clear: when we say that he carried our suffering, this does not mean that he put an end to our suffering by taking it all on himself. He does not *substitute* himself for us in our diseases, torments, and griefs. He does not leave us impassive and unscathed. Suffering always remains horrible, for it is an insult to the order of creation (but not of "nature").

TO BE ACCOMPANIED

What is changed is changed in two ways. First of all, there is a change in suffering in that, if we believe, we should know and even feel that we are no longer alone in this suffering. Someone else is suffering along with me, like me, next to me. How often we say that "one always dies alone"; in the same way, so many of us have experienced that suffering separates us from others. Even those who love us are strangers to our suffering. This psychological experience worsens our ordeal. Through faith, we are joined in our most profound suffering and distress by "the one who carried," and

I should know that it is precisely *my* suffering that he bears as I am bearing it. I have a true companion in suffering, a companion who bears and shares this horror, this pain, this grief, this desertion. All I need to do is turn to him and find once again my communion with him; the opening occurs; and I then am accompanied in truth. Thus, I suffer less because I am not alone. So many of us have experienced this ourselves and seen it in others. When you are with a dying person, the simple act of holding his hand makes the agony less tormenting. To have a simple human friend is already an incomparable hope, so imagine, the Son of God . . . But you must believe with all your heart.

LIBERATED

There is a second modification in regard to our suffering. Whether we are conscious of it or not, suffering is always more or less experienced as a punishment. In everyday speech we often say, "What have I done to God to make him send me this misfortune?" All those who suffer have the same anxiety in one way or another. One person will connect the suffering to a youthful mistake; another will see it as a terrible injustice to which he has fallen victim; another will understand it as a condemnation of his whole life . . . This way of thinking is never completely absent from our suffering. Now, in God's revelation, we learn—and in faith we are called to live out—the truth that anything having to do with condemnation is taken out of our misfortune because another has taken the *whole* condemnation and all *our* condemnations upon himself. As far as condemnation linked to suffering is concerned, he did indeed substitute himself for us. Suffering remains naked.

Of course, suffering will persist as long as the world is the world and as long as men have not been "renewed"—but from now on, it is "naked," that is, it has no ultimate "cause." There is no reason for it, and I am not spiritually responsible for it. God does not intervene in my suffering to cause it or to punish me and neither does he use it to purify me! Jesus took care of all this for me. So suffering is purely the playing out of material forces; it comes from germs or enemies, from accidents or mistakes. In other words, it has no meaning; it is absurd. Because anything that was part of the "non-absurdity" of this suffering, its deep meaning, was borne by Jesus and Jesus alone. So I need to live this *first of all* as a fact. It should never be experienced as condemnation.

Yet, as a man, I cannot help thinking about this suffering and cannot help questioning it. Perhaps I will be able *to find* some meaning, to give it some positive value, or to receive it as a challenge to be overcome . . . In that case, I am doing something good. That is normal. In other words, I need to transform into a positive condition that which diminishes me or reduces me. This, of course, is not against God's will! What we must exclude, though, is the dread of punishment, of remorse, of judgment, and of wrong-doing: we need to know that we have been liberated from those things. However, we should welcome all the rest—the attempt to integrate suffering and misfortune into the totality of my life and turn it into an active and invigorating component of my being! It is a good thing not to seek to live outside or against our limits and our pain. We should certainly do it without any illusions as to the frailty of the human condition. Yet, we must always remember that henceforth the human condition has been liberated, so people can bear suffering with greatness and with humility. He can do it so much more *truly* when he knows that God himself bore evil in himself.

The Various Sufferings of Jesus: Hunger

I have said that we need to take into consideration the most humble suffering of Jesus. The Gospels often speak of it. For example, Jesus was hungry. We are told this explicitly after Jesus fasted in the desert for forty days (Matt 4:2). In another text, when Jesus is confronted with so many requests (and especially requests for healing), hunger is alluded to: "Then, because so many people were coming and going that they did not even have a chance to eat"

(Mark 6:31). On another occasion, when Jesus arrived at Bethany for his final journey to Jerusalem, Mark tells us that he was hungry (11:12). Of course, in each of these instances, the purpose of the text is not primarily to inform us that he was hungry. However, we should not neglect this detail, nor should we dismiss his cry of "I am thirsty" during the crucifixion (John 19:28). John tells us that these words were spoken so that all Scripture might be fulfilled. Granted, but let us not forget that at that very moment, like any crucified person, he was actually thirsty. So of course, he experienced this human weakness—to be hungry and to be thirsty—and *genuinely* did so. Let us now pause and consider the first thought.

After forty days in the desert without eating, Jesus was hungry. We know from the experience of people who have gone on hunger strikes that forty days of fasting is the limit of what a person can bear. Of course, some will say (and as I myself have written on several occasions) that the number forty is symbolic. Yet, for the remainder of the passage to make sense, there must have been some concrete reality making Jesus very hungry. It is indeed immediately after this that the devil appears to him and tempts him by suggesting that he transform stones into bread. Obviously, the Jesus whom the Gospels describe could have worked that miracle and thus could have had plenty of bread. It is important for the Gospel writer to remind us that Jesus was *really* very hungry. Otherwise there would have been no temptation. Jesus was really tempted on this most humble physical level. He was hungry. This reminds us that Jesus experienced all the temptations arising from physical needs, just as any person does. We shall return to this later.

Jesus refuses to perform this miracle. It is his first refusal to perform a miracle. Why does he refuse? Was it because the suggestion came from the devil? As I have stated before, the devil is not a person in my understanding. Rather, the temptation comes from the fact that Jesus is experiencing an urgent need to eat and that he commands power that would enable him to satisfy his hunger. In fact, Jesus sees in this temptation to perform a miracle an action of the "dia-bolos," the one who separates, the one who would have separated him from God. Why? This is because if he had performed the miracle, it would first of all have been a miracle performed *in his own interest*. Jesus never performed miracles *for himself* because he came to bear witness to a love for which he will sacrifice himself.

He will never use his power for himself; quite the contrary, where he is concerned, he offers himself up in non-power. Furthermore, this miracle consisting of turning stones into bread would have been a typical example of the *marvelous*. We see many times that Jesus never gave in to the "pleasure" of doing marvelous things. The miracles of Jesus have nothing to do with the works of magicians, sorcerers, and so on . . . They *all* come from his love of others and of the Father. To turn stones into bread, to turn lead into gold, to make clay birds and blow on them to give them life (as in the Infancy Gospels), to make a table laden with delicious foods come down from heaven (as in the Koran)—these are miracles that Jesus always *refused* to perform. His miracles are the miracles of love, never the miracles of power, of show, of publicity, and so on.[1]

Not by Bread Alone

So Jesus is hungry and he refuses to satisfy this hunger through a miracle. He does not, however, refuse to satisfy the hunger *of others* by performing a miracle in the feeding of the multitude. The answer he gives to his own hunger—perfectly physiological hunger—is that people shall not *live* by bread *alone* but by the Word of God.

He does not deny that people need bread when faced with hunger, but he affirms that this nourishment is not sufficient (even

1. The wrong that he was induced to commit was to take over the power of God (which is in him and which the Father gives him) to satisfy his own needs, even legitimate needs, and turn the power toward himself. This is actually a fundamental theological question because it contains all creation! Did God create to satisfy himself, or did he do so out of love so as to answer the temptation of nothingness and of divine selfishness?

while indispensable), and that to satisfy the *totality* of human hunger, the Word of God is necessary. So he will wait for the Word to feed him. The text ends by reporting that "the angels ministered to him." This is obviously a reference to Elijah, yet Elijah was served by angels *before* his forty-day journey in the desert. If God feeds people in their complete being (which we often translate as "soul"), we can be assured that when they are fed by the Word they will also be satisfied in their material hunger. This first example clearly shows the relationship between suffering and temptation and also the truly human character of Jesus, who shared everything human in suffering, both great and small.

FATIGUE

Similarly, we often encounter Jesus being *tired*. Here again, we should not imagine a "super nature" that would make him a tireless walker! At the time of the violent storm on the Sea of Galilee, Jesus was sleeping. For him to be asleep during that storm, he had to have been tired. He also reminds people that the Son of Man has no place to lay his head. Clearly, he is referring to his controversial situation but also inseparably to his exhausting wanderings. John explicitly tells us that Jesus, as he was returning to Galilee and crossing Samaria, sat down because he was tired.

TORTURE AND CRUCIFIXION

Of course, as we consider the physical humanity of Christ, with its limitations and suffering, we must not neglect what is always emphasized: the arrest, the blows, the crown of thorns, and the crucifixion. So much has been said about them that I will only mention them here. While we will not consider them on their own, we must nevertheless take them very seriously in this meditation on the humanity of Jesus in sharing our weaknesses and our suffering.

Moral Suffering

We will now enter into new areas of suffering. To those who have never thought of suffering beyond the cross, this might appear risky or even slightly blasphemous because we will consider psychological or moral suffering. Nevertheless, as a doctor specializing in pain has said, "Suffering is a total suffering that not only includes physical pain but also psychological, social, and spiritual factors. Dividing up a *whole* and distressing *experience* into pieces is a little artificial, but it has nonetheless helped me to understand ... the patients."[2]

Rupture

First of all, we see the rupture with his "environment," the breaking of family ties. His relatives consider him insane. "When his family heard about this, they went to take charge of him, for they said, 'He is out of his mind.'" (Mark 3:7). For "even his own brothers did not believe in him" (John 7:5) and asked him to go away! He felt this rejection deeply and uttered these words, which are actually very bitter: "Only in his hometown, among his relatives and in his own house is a prophet without honor." I have often heard this phrase quoted lightly! Yet for him, whose mother knew the miracle of his birth and of his childhood, what suffering it must have been to be part of a "house" that despised him. In Luke, the phrase is slightly softened: "No prophet is accepted in his hometown." Mathew, on the contrary, adds that "He did not do many miracles there because of their lack of faith." Later, he will meet those who have hardened hearts.

We are now entering a very delicate sphere: Jesus *perceives* that he is rejected by his family members, who do not believe his words and do not believe in his vocation, that is, his very being. Although we cannot imagine that there is any resentment or desire for vengeance in the words, this situation leads him to utter the famous

2. Saunders, "Hospice, lieu de rencontre pour la Science et la religion."

phrase, "Who are my mother and my brothers?" His mother and his brothers then arrived. Standing outside, they sent someone in to call him" (perhaps this is the same situation as above . . . they came to take away this insane and sacrilegious person). "They told him: 'Your mother and brothers are outside looking for you.' Then he looked at those seated in a circle around him and said: 'Here are my mother and my brothers! For whoever does God's will is my brother and sister and mother'" (Mark 3:31–35). This passage is always interpreted to show the importance that Jesus gives to faith, which can create bonds as strong as those within a family. Is it not also possible to understand it as his break with his family because that family had rejected him? How could we believe that this break did not cause dreadful suffering to the one who was the incarnation of love? His family did not accept him. The breach was a fact. He does not oppose any of it because what is important is to do the will of his father in heaven.[3] When one thinks about the fact that this man experienced everything that the average person experiences but in an absolute way, in the most total, the most complete, and the most conscious way, we can imagine his suffering when he was forced to choose between the most precious human bonds and the will of the Father. How could he not have suffered infinitely as he said, "Who are my brothers and my mother?"

Yet, he now knows that it is not possible to obey both, that is, it is not possible to do the complete will of the Father by staying peacefully and comfortably nestled in the earthly affection of his family. So he will go beyond and make this choice into a kind of rule for his disciples: "Whoever loves his father or mother more than me is not worthy of me" (Matt 10:37), and, "A man's enemies will be the members of his own household." In Luke, he will even be harsher: "If anyone comes to me and does not hate his father and

---

3. There might even be a foreshadowing of this break with his family in the famous passage about Jesus as a twelve-year-old with his parents in Jerusalem for the Passover (Luke 2:41–50). He leaves them, and they anxiously search for him while he is in the Temple with the doctors of the Law. "Didn't you know that I had to be in my father's house?" is the answer to his mother's worried question. The break is already fully there.

mother, his wife and children, his brothers and sisters, *he cannot be my disciple*" (14:26). What suffering he must have experienced in order to go so far. Let there be no confusion: This is not some kind of sadistic commandment, not a "test." It is the exact counterpart of, the answer to, and the reversal of what John proclaims: "The world hates me and you will be hated by the world." That is the starting point. This also includes suffering for Jesus. Certainly, he does not ask to repay hatred with hatred; but he knows that there is an absolute choice to make between the will of his Father and the wills of this world. He sees that men hate him and, consequently, they also hate the Father. Right from the start, he warns his disciples that there is a price to pay: if you choose God (and me), you will be hated by all and will have to make a break with what you love and those you love in this world!

How far the study of the suffering of Jesus takes us from that comfortable institution Christendom, how far from the comfortable Christian bourgeoisie. We shall see him apply this inevitable choice concretely when he tells the man who asks for time to go and bury his father: Let the dead bury their dead. He even questions what was considered the most sacred family duties. Is this inhuman? Not at all, for in the break that is made so that we may choose the Father and follow Jesus, a new love is born for the very persons with whom we had broken. We love them differently and in a perfect way in the actual pain of separation. It is not a rejection leading to perdition but a break for salvation and for leading to love in its complete form. Yet, how we must suffer to enter upon this path! For Jesus, there is already absolute suffering here. He becomes, as do those who follow him, someone who is uprooted and maladjusted, without any established or definitive place in any society. He did away with affections, earthly loves, rites, hierarchies, moral imperatives. . . .

Can we believe that such a thing was easy for him? That which is already difficult for the average person was infinitely more so for the person who was *any and all* love incarnate—contrary to what a superficial understanding might suggest in thinking of him as a superman. In order to complete this break, this wrenching apart, he says, "Do not suppose that I have come to bring peace to the earth. I did not come to bring peace but a sword" (Matt 10:34); and "Do you think I came to bring peace on earth? No, I tell you, but division. From now on there will be five in one family divided against each other, three against two and two against three. They will be divided father against son and son against father, mother against daughter and daughter against mother" (Luke 12:51–53). Let us not be mistaken here: He did indeed come to bring peace ("Peace, I give to you. My peace I give to you"). He came *in order for* this to happen—he is the one through whom all reconciliation is accomplished. Yet, against the Father's plan and against his own will, the world refuses this peace and condemns those who listen to this word. Jesus did not come in order to divide the world and to cause these breaks, but division occurs because of his very presence and through his word. The real presence of Jesus inevitably causes the breaks from which he is the first to suffer. Imagine the suffering of Jesus as he saw around him the exact opposite of what he would have wanted and of what he had proclaimed. We can already see the first fruits here, and Jesus has to acknowledge his failure. Where he wanted peace, there is division, fracture, and hatred. The failure of all our good intentions, of all our great projects, and of all our good sentiments is here borne by him who was acquainted with all human suffering.

He Bore Our Suffering

At this point, a very awkward and worrisome text comes to mind: Jesus went to the home of Peter and cured the apostle's mother-in-law and other sick people. Matthew says, "This was to fulfill what was spoken through the prophet Isaiah: 'He took up our infirmities and carried our diseases'" (Matt 8:17). Of course, the Greek text could be translated as "has taken our infirmities away, removed our disease"; and then the person of Jesus would not be in play: he healed just as a healer does. Is this really the meaning? The text in Isaiah (53:3) seems to say that the Messiah bears on himself our suffering and carries our diseases himself.[4] This would of course change our perspective and our understanding. Jesus is no longer a healer who comes along doing good: he takes onto himself the evil that he heals. He is thus wholly participating in our suffering and our misery. He does much more than relieve it from the outside: he takes onto himself the evil that was striking us. I know that this will scandalize many: in a strange way, we are perfectly willing to accept this from a spiritual point of view (Jesus takes our sin onto himself); but if we say that he becomes blind as he heals a blind person, we shrug our shoulders and think that it makes no sense. It means that for us, a material action is much more important than a spiritual action. It means that the "idea" of Jesus carrying our sins remains a vague and imprecise "idea" and that the specificity of a material disease leaves us unbelieving.

Of course, when I listen to this text respectfully, I do not believe that it tells me that Jesus became materially blind by healing a blind person or materially sick by healing a leper or a lame person. What it says is that Jesus takes onto himself all the suffering of the blind person as a blind person or the suffering of the leper as a leper, without necessarily having all the exterior signs of the affliction. There is an essential transference of the disease from one person to the other. In this, he is really participating in and really taking onto himself all our sicknesses. This is why the miracle does not need to become universal: when Jesus heals a leper, Jesus suffers from the suffering *of* the leper and owing to that, he suffers *for* all lepers. As far as the material healing is concerned, it is the result of his love and compassion for a person that he meets, and that is in fact a different story. It is essential to remember that all the suffering of all *our diseases* is included in the suffering of Jesus.

4. This translation is confirmed and even reinforced by Chouraqui's translation of the verses that follow.

Experiencing His Limits

Whether Jesus had knowledge of, was aware of, his divinity is a theological question that is unresolvable; neither facts nor arguments will enable us to answer it. However, the texts do give us indications that he was aware of his weakness—and in fact, did he not come into the world to represent the "weakness" of God and his limits? Are these real limits or limits that he set for himself, as during his arrest when he declared that if he wanted, he could have summoned twelve legions of angels? This again is a question that we cannot answer. Be that as it may, it is certain that this knowledge caused suffering as well as temptation, the temptation to go beyond this weakness.

Let us look at some examples: "'Good teacher' a man asked . . . 'Why do you call me good? No one is good except God alone'" (Mark 10:18). Jesus sharply cuts off the temptation that is presented, the temptation to assimilate himself to the Father. Yet, he also said, "I and the Father are one." Yes, but Jesus does not want to attribute to himself that which, as he recognizes, only belongs to the Father. He, Jesus, is not good: men must recognize only God as being good. Jesus gives back to and commends to the Father everything that is attributed to him. He does not recognize himself as good, or rather, he does not want to turn the love of men toward him and refuses to be good. Only the Father has in himself all the goodness of the universe, and only the Father can *say* what is good (a power that Adam wanted to possess); and the Creator pronounces the blessing for each day of his creation: "He saw his work, and he saw that all of it was good."

Personal Weaknesses

Beyond this fundamental decision, Jesus knew apparent moments of weakness or uncertainty. We have already seen that at some point he was unable to perform miracles because of unbelief. In the same way, when the Pharisees came to see him to ask for a "sign," we see the issue of Jesus' refusal to perform a miracle for the sake of astonishing or convincing—and Jesus does not even try! "Why does this generation ask for a miraculous sign? . . . I tell you the truth, no sign will be given to it" (Mark 8:12). And this generation is not only the generation of his times, every generation of humanity always asks for proofs and signs!

Finally, it is necessary to take Jesus' own uncertainties into consideration in this weakness. Yes, we must do so once more, and let us remember that he is not a superman, he is not an "omniscient clairvoyant." He said, "Watch out that no one deceives you. For many will come in my name claiming: I am he. Do not follow them." What will happen *after him* . . . Jesus does not seem to know. He then asks a question full of anguish: "However, when the Son of Man comes, will he find faith on the earth?" (Luke 8:18). Jesus does not seem to know, to have any certainty, about the duration of the fire he is lighting, about the trustworthiness of his disciples, or about the continuation of the work.

We must consider whether he is actually expressing a deep conviction or if these are "teaching devices"! For Jesus could have said these things to admonish us to be vigilant or to show us our responsibility. That is, it depends on us as to whether faith will continue from generation to generation and remain alive so that the Son of Man, when he appears, finds faith alive—that is, a witness to the fact that his immense sacrifice was not made in vain. This is the meaning of these two texts, and it corresponds to the command: "Watch."

Jesus was not a teacher. He was not a Socrates posing questions to help others move on. Everything he says is said and *lived the same way*. We must therefore understand these texts as real questions that Jesus was asking himself. As long as he was there with his disciples, he could, as the shepherd, correct the situation. But what will happen afterward? He offers no guarantees, for he does not know how long there will be faithfulness. He does not know who will succeed this first group of disciples that he trained, how they will transmit the revealed Word—the gospel, how they will resist all the claims of future messiahs[5] or for how many gen-

5. Let us remember this text to counter the claim of Mohammed, to whom it applies.

erations. For Jesus does not know how long this history will last. The only answer we have, the one that, on the one hand, should put an end to all our speculation and, on the other, shows the limit that Jesus recognizes so as not to encroach upon the Father is well known: "But about that day and hour no one knows, not even . . . the Son, but only the Father."

SENSITIVITY

Jesus also manifested a great sensitivity, being distressed like any other person. This is not a weakness and it is not sentimentality either: he continues to share everything in the human condition, and just like the best of us, he suffers when faced with misfortune and suffers for the misfortune of others. "He had compassion" is a phrase we read so many times. Once again let us be clear that this is not an all-powerful God who from the height of his power and his immateriality shows compassion, as Victor Hugo had compassion on the toad.[6] No, when Jesus has compassion, it is as a man among men. There are two differences, however: his compassion is total, and it is lasting. His is a total compassion, whereas we are affected by various feelings that divide us; and among those feelings, there is *also* compassion. All of him is in his compassion precisely because he is God-with-man. His is a durable compassion, not the fleeting emotion we feel when we see the starving children of Ethiopia or Sudan and then proceed to forget as soon as we see something else. Jesus does not forget, for God continually remembers.

JESUS AND THE CROWD

"When he saw the crowds, he had compassion on them because they were harassed and helpless, like sheep without a shepherd" (Matt 9:36). These words follow directly upon the story of Jesus

6. [Ellul is referring to "Le Crapaud" (the Toad), a well-known poem by the French writer Victor Hugo.]

healing all the sick that were brought to him. There are no individual cases nor any specific diseases cited here. This is an example of something else, something very familiar to us: it is a man in a crowd, a man among the masses, the man of crowds, who is nothing more than a member of the crowd. This is our condition as a result of population growth and the hell of cities. Jesus had already *seen* what this would mean, and he had compassion because this conglomeration has no meaning, no value, and no direction. They are harassed and helpless because the crowd has no reason within itself, no truth, and no word. Nor do they have a shepherd. This is the *Crux viarum*, the crossroads! For this crowd is at the mercy of the first shepherd who comes along, at the mercy of the evil shepherd—the Duce, the Führer, the tsar. It is not only the present misery of the crowd that fills Jesus with compassion, but it is the potential for horror that it contains when the evil shepherd takes the lead. It is this future of the crowd that fills Jesus with compassion.

Here again, we have one more paradox in the ever surprising behavior of Jesus, for he does not take the lead. He does not say to the crowd, those who are together, harassed, sad, and disoriented, "Follow me, for *I* am the good shepherd." He does not because, unfortunately, he knows that if he starts leading the crowd, taking charge of it, and directing it, he will, by *the very act of doing so*, become an evil shepherd. By leading a crowd, he would dispossess each person of his own individuality a little bit more and would confirm the crowd in its "being a crowd," in its nonexistence, in its lack of value and meaning. Of course, he will say, "I am the good shepherd." *But to whom does he say it?* Does he say it to the harassed crowd to make it acknowledge him? Not at all! He says it to those who should have been good shepherds, to those who instead of taking advantage of the crowd should have kept it from turning into a crowd, to those who should have brought such a word of truth that each one would have found meaning, truth, and life and would not have vainly sought an illusory consolation in gathering together.

These are terrible words for us who live in a mass society and witness the tragic phenomenon of the mass that is satisfied in being itself and in being this way. "To be many" today is the only way of "being"! Jesus is filled with compassion for this mad society. What does he do? According to the texts, he does not do anything directly. He will only send his first missionaries. He will not send them to supervise the crowd but rather, I will say, to dissolve it! He says two things to his disciples: heal the sick and proclaim that the Kingdom of heaven is at hand. He asks them on the one hand to individualize misfortune and on the other to give direction, meaning, and orientation. There is then no more crowd—all the less so as the apostles' work is individualized! The crowd will cease to be a crowd, the man in the crowd will cease to be despondent, "suicidal," and without any reason for being. There is a reason for being. But no leader will ever supply the reason for being that actually causes being. So Jesus is distraught, like a man who witnesses a military force advancing toward death.

COMPASSION FOR JERUSALEM

As Jesus is filled with compassion, he experiences total compassion, not only for the crowd but also for individuals (see, for example, Luke 7:13); and this is directly connected to the emotion he feels in the face of any suffering. It is his compassion for Jerusalem that I would like to consider: "Jerusalem, Jerusalem, you kill the prophets and stone those sent to you, how often I have longed to gather your children together, as a hen gathers her chicks under her wings, but you were not willing! Look, your house is left to you desolate. For I tell you, you will not see me again until you say, 'Blessed is he who comes in the name of the Lord'" (Matt 23:37–39). These are not words of anger or the final words of condemnation. Jesus knows that Jerusalem is the place chosen by the God of Israel, by his God, as his "dwelling place" and the place to gather all the peoples of the earth. However, Jerusalem wanted to seize for itself a privilege; she refused God's calls and rejected Jesus. The welcome given on Palm Sunday will not change anything. From now on, the people of Israel are divided even in Jerusalem: scribes, Pharisees, Essenes, Sadducees, Zealots, Herodians. . . .

Jesus wanted to be the one who gathered. It was not possible. Instead, he was rejected by all. The gathering he wanted was not the gathering of triumph, of glory, but the *protective* gathering, "as a hen gathers her chicks." Now, because it refused this ultimate help, Jerusalem will be empty, deserted. What does that mean? First of all, let me say once again that it is not a condemnation that Jesus pronounces on the city. He announces what will happen and states what will occur. Nothing more. He does not say that the inhabitants will be driven away; no, *your* house *will be* left for you; but it will be *desolate*. That is, God will no longer dwell there because Jerusalem rejected the last one sent by God, his very Son. Henceforth, although Jerusalem will still be inhabited, it will be a city emptied of its meaning, a city without glory, without truth. So Jesus weeps over Jerusalem, much more than over himself! For like any pious Jew, he loves Jerusalem more than himself.

This interpretation is confirmed in Luke, according to whom Jesus speaks three times of Jerusalem (13:34; 19:41–44; and 23:28). "As he approached Jerusalem and saw the city, he *wept* over it." He weeps out of suffering not only because of the dark future that he can see for his country but because Jerusalem no longer knows its very being: "If you, even you, had only known *on this day* (the day of the coming of Jesus, of the actual coming of God into his city) what would *bring* you peace . . ." The peace whose name it bears. What would bring peace! The peace that rests on you and in you. What would bring you peace (or in another translation: the way of your peace), the way that Jesus shows, which is the surest way and also the way that *expresses* the peace of Jerusalem. Yet, the absolute city, the only blessed city, the only city beloved of God did not fulfill what was expected of her. And so Jesus weeps over the city and also weeps over this new failure of God's plan. The rest, the prediction that Jerusalem will be finally destroyed (which, according to positivist historians, must have been written *after* the conquest of Jerusalem by Titus), is only the normal consequence of what is happening: if it is true that Jerusalem rejected God in his Son, then she has no more historical role to play; and her enemies will triumph over her in a "normal" manner. Jesus comes back to this theme, not regarding Jerusalem, but concerning the women of Jerusalem as he is taken to the place of crucifixion: "Daughters of Jerusalem, do not weep for me; weep for yourselves and for your children." So the passionate love of Jesus for Jerusalem and its inhabitants causes him greater suffering than the fear of the torture that is to come. This was a constant suffering for the Son of Man in addition to all his other suffering.

Woe unto You, Scribes!

If he grieves over the indifference of Jerusalem, over a Jerusalem that does not recognize the one who was sent to her, Jesus also grieves over those who are hostile to him. The woes that he pronounces over the Pharisees and the scribes are not, let us remember, a curse, a sign of combat or of hatred on his part! Remember: God so loved the world . . . Jesus cannot have acted or spoken out of hatred, he cannot have condemned: here again, he *announces* that there is going to be a serious misfortune. Misfortune will come and strike you. So be careful! This is what all the prophets did. This is confirmed for us in passages such as the following: Is it permissible to do good and heal on the Sabbath? No one answers him. "He looked at them in anger *and deeply distressed* at their stubborn hearts." He is angry that scrupulous and literal obedience to the law makes it impossible to answer the simple question of whether one can do good on the Sabbath. In other words, this obedience smothers compassion and a simple sense of humanity. He is angry but at the same time also unhappy, distressed, and saddened. How is it possible not to have pity on a sick man? Yet, even though he is distressed by the hardness of their hearts, he does not judge them. He grieves for them, for those who are the people of God and his people. How is it possible to interpret the will of

God as exclusion and refusal to help? "And he was amazed at their hardness of heart" (Mark 6:6).[7]

Finally, in this gamut of emotions, of sensitive suffering, Jesus experiences great anguish. This is not first of all anguish about his coming death—which we will encounter later—but anguish over the work that the Father sent him to accomplish. We find enigmatic texts: "But I have a baptism to undergo, and how distressed I am until it is completed" (or "I have to undergo an immersion"—this would mean a plunge into death—"and how oppressed I am by the concern that it must be accomplished." This is Hubert Pernot's translation). He would like it to be past, for he knows what a terrible ordeal it will be; we find the same idea in the passage about the fire that he must light and the rupture he must cause within families and among friends. Thus, it is not only his own personal destiny that plunges him into anguish, but also the consequences of his work, that which will inevitably follow his preaching, and even more the exclusion of God from among men.

STUMBLING BLOCKS

I would connect this anguish to the pronouncement on stumbling. I am well aware that what follows will seem unthinkable to the reader accustomed to the usual interpretation: "And he said unto his disciples, 'It is inevitable that stumbling blocks (snares) come; but woe to him through whom they come! It would be better for him if a millstone were hung about his neck, and he were thrown into the sea, rather than that he should cause one of these little ones to stumble. *Be on your guard*,'"[8] says Jesus. If this referred to stumbling blocks caused in many places in the world by the rich, the powerful, the immoral, and the evil, it would be a trivial statement: those who cause the humble to stumble will be punished. It really was not necessary for Jesus to say that! What is the relationship of this to the last admonition Jesus gives his disciples: "Be on

7. [This is Ellul's own translation of Mark 6:6.]

8. New American Standard Version.

your guard"? It would not make sense to tell them: "Be on your guard!" No, the clear meaning of the text is: "You may be the bearers of stumbling blocks; your word can become a snare for the little ones. Be careful." But at the same time, he says, "It is inevitable that stumbling blocks come!" What stumbling blocks? Any stumbling block? Of course not. Jesus speaks about himself, of this fire that he lights, and of the conflicts that he causes by his very presence, by his preaching, by his miracles, by his "unveiling." How could he avoid stumbling blocks when he said "Son of God" and "I and the Father are One" and when he was proclaimed "the Messiah of Israel"? How could this not become a snare first of all for the true believers of Israel? "I cannot help creating stumbling blocks. But I also know that this will have terrible consequences."

He is not concerned with the consequences or afraid of them, but he worries about the little ones. He is in anguish and saddened because of them, because they also might fall into a snare; and Jesus is unable to keep this revelation from being a snare. It is necessarily a stumbling block. How is it possible to believe, how can anyone believe without fear and trembling that all of God was present in a man? Who can believe that God incarnate is dying on a cross? No reasonable being can accept such an implausible and frightening revelation, the impact of which always makes one reassess everything. The stumbling block of Jesus is inevitable, and he knows it will happen and pronounces over himself, "Woe unto him, through whom the occasion of stumbling comes." He says it about himself, for himself, and sees that it will last for millennia.

The greatest of all stumbling blocks is realized when one group, one church, or one people no longer finds this unbearable revelation to be a stumbling block. The greatest of all snares, as Søren Kierkegaard showed, is for the Incarnation and the Crucifixion simply to become natural realities. Jesus suffers for all of those for whom he will be a snare and a stumbling block. Yet, we must understand that neither would he be the savior that he is if he were not an occasion of stumbling. He would not be the Way, the Truth, and the Life. And for the sake of the little ones, this abyss makes him tremble.

The Apostles

In this long wandering through the everyday suffering of Jesus, we now come to his closest circle: the disciples and the apostles themselves. Even they—although they believed him, followed him, and confessed who he was—even they caused him suffering. He suffered in his human friendship for them. He suffered because of their incomprehension, which was the failure of his teaching. (What? You do not understand this parable? How will you ever understand all that happens in parables?) He suffered from having to leave the Father's absolute truth in such fragile hands. He suffered from misunderstandings, which the Gospel of John so often recounts. He suffered both in his affections and in truth. Let us remember all those familiar texts.

Get behind Me, Satan!

As soon as Peter makes his great confession, which is in the hearts of all the apostles, he doubts the word of Jesus and becomes for him an occasion of temptation! "This is not possible; you are not going to stick your head into the lion's mouth!" Then, "Get behind me Satan; you are a snare for me." Can we believe that Jesus could have said these words to Peter, the faithful one, the enthusiastic one, the one who "was ready for anything," without suffering as he had to reject in this way the most faithful and apparently the most reliable friend? For when Jesus says "Satan" (accuser) to someone, he does not do so lightly. Who then is Peter accusing? Simply God! Jesus has just told them that the will of God is that he should be handed over and be put to death! When Peter declares, "It is impossible!" he is implicitly accusing God . . . as we so often do. At this point, Jesus suffers with the Father and suffers from the fact that this same Peter, who had evinced true discernment, utters such an outrageously foolish thing the next minute. The disciples have been with him for two years, and Jesus notes that they are still unbelieving, even after all they have experienced with him, after all they have seen and heard. . . .

Unbelief

They have been called by a father to heal his son. They have not been able to do so. We hear two terrible words when the disciples recount their inability to heal. First of all: "O, unbelieving and perverse generation, how long shall I put up with you?" Jesus is infuriated by this human environment, in which he encounters only unbelief. No one wants to believe in this Father God who answers a true prayer of faith. This time, it is not an attack on the "hypocritical scribes and Pharisees"; all those who are present are addressed. So we are forced to link unbelief with perversity. This goes deeper that simple "immorality." It is perverse, perverted, and fundamentally evil by deviating in the direction of hypocrisy. Jesus finds it difficult to put up with them, and he would much prefer to be alone, out of this rotten world whose inability to heal reveals the absence of faith and the presence of perversity. He is almost discouraged in front of this mountain that must be moved.

We need to hear this exclamation of anger and suffering with great seriousness because it is not intended for the Jews but for us. What is it that reveals our fundamental unbelief and perversity? Not the simple fact that we cannot heal a sick person by prayer but, much more generally, the fact that *we cannot heal*. We cannot heal our mad world of its folly. We cannot heal the thirst for money or power, heal ourselves of the technological-scientific spiral, or heal the natural world, this garden given to us. Unbelieving and perverted: that is what *we* are in this world, which itself is unbelieving and perverted. Today, we need to heed this cry, and we Christians especially need to heed it. The rest of the text proves this. After speaking to the crowd, Jesus again says to his questioning disciples: "You could not do anything because of your lack of faith." He is talking to us, to us Christians, without exception. We should be the first ones capable of initiating the healing of this world, to heal it of its *hubris* and of its despair, which sometimes falls into water and sometimes into fire! And we can do nothing. Or rather, each time a Church starts something, it is certain to be wrong, because it has not centered *everything* on faith and started with faith—faith is such a trivial thing among Christians that we do not even need to speak of it any longer!

If you had faith like a mustard seed . . . the mountain would be moved. Let us observe that Jesus never moved any mountains to provide entertainment or to prove "his faith"! He only says this to his disciples to show them (us) the mediocrity, the vanity, and the insignificance of "our" faith. "Nothing would be impossible for you." Instead, *everything* is impossible for us! We do not know how to witness in truth or love in truth or manifest the extraordinary abundance of the grace of God. We can neither forgive nor heal. Here, we are up against the wall.

Could we believe that Jesus said these words lightly? How much it must have cost him! "How long shall I stay with you?" As if he were regretting the decision made by the Father and the Son that required the latter to empty himself to come and live among men. He has had enough. What suffering and discouragement this expresses. What an assessment of failure! Yet, since that moment, Jesus continues to put up with us! "I am with you always . . ." Our unbelief and our perversity nevertheless continue to cause him suffering, as does our inability, as Christians, to heal anything in this sick world.

FRIENDS

Certainly, Jesus suffers from having unbelieving disciples, yet they remain his friends, his faithful . . . but the drama is going to manifest itself also on the simply human plane. In fact, it is not true that his disciples (that is, we) have any friendship, simply human friendship, for this venerated Master. The series of abandonments and denials prove it. In the end, he remains alone, abandoned by all, having lost all, both at the "spiritual" level and at the level of a simple human relationship. He lost them all except one companion, the other crucified man, the one who made a confession of faith that might be more essential than the confession made by Peter.

GETHSEMANE

This abandonment starts during the night in Gethsemane when the apostles sleep. We all remember this dramatic story. Jesus goes off a little ways to pray. Perhaps one reason he does this is so that the disciples might not see the depth of his despair, his discouragement, and his fear. Is it fear of death? Perhaps, perhaps not. Because he knows that this death will reveal his abandonment. He also knows that he will be alone, without the Father. This break frightens him, certainly more than the actual torture. This abandonment starts with the apostles' sleep: "Could you men not keep watch for one hour?" In addition to the discouragement of having disciples with so little vigilance, there is another fear, the fear that his disciples might be so weak, so inattentive, so lacking in courage that they might let everything go once Jesus is no longer there. To the reproach about not having accompanied him in his watch of struggle and submission, he therefore adds the warning, "Watch and pray so that you will not fall into temptation." Which temptation does he mean? It is the temptation to let everything go, to sleep instead of pursuing the work of their Lord, and to be unable to carry the gospel to others. Watch and pray! This is exactly what they did not do. His reproach and his exhortation are of no use. When he comes back, he finds them asleep again. What abandonment! No man has ever been so forsaken, for it is not only the absence of a friend or a brother but the absence of *any* spiritual help and the proof of the frailty of those on whom he was counting. He does not doubt their friendship, their . . . faith, and yet, "the spirit is willing, but the flesh is weak." It is so weak that at the most terrible moment (he has just told them, "My soul is overwhelmed with sorrow to the point of death," and that has not kept them awake!)—the flesh wins out in a most trivial way (the need for sleep). How will it be when the Master is no longer there?

Mark ends this terrible scene with a phrase that is ironic and perhaps a little bitter. As Jesus finds them asleep a third time, he says, "Sleep now, rest. It is settled, the hour has come, the Son of Man is betrayed." This is a terrible statement: "I really cannot count on you. I will go alone to this death. So go ahead and rest. It is no longer time to pray to God with me." Perhaps we could even read between the lines: "If you had watched and prayed, if you had come with me and supported me in this struggle, if we had been united together, then perhaps God would have relented. Perhaps destiny would not have played out. It is over. I must now fulfill the will of the Father, which despite everything, remains the will of the Father. But you will not participate in its fulfillment. You left me alone, go on now. Sleep now! This phrase echoes all the way to us. It is spoken to the church, the church of sleep, in all times—institutional sleep, spiritualistic sleep (flight into mystic clouds), sleep through entertainment with a hundred different passionate activities (political or otherwise), activist sleep (in dreams), fundamentalist sleep (when the Bible becomes the pillow of sloth because all we need to do is read it word-for-word!). The sleep of churches corresponds exactly to this derision. "Sleep now because everything is settled!" This abandonment in Gethsemane announces and prefigures all others. One has often contrasted the betrayal of Judas and the denial of Peter: That is correct, one is not worse than the other. The church has often given a strange judgment in the case, by traditionally making Judas the cursed one and Peter . . . the first pope! He who says aloud, "I do not know him; I do not know who this man is"—does he not know who the one he proclaimed to be the Son of God is? Jesus knew that Peter would deny him. The flesh is weak: In this climate of terror, Peter simply became afraid. Nothing can redeem such a denial except the grace given to the one who repents. Peter does not know yet. His denial also reflects his distress: Everything is lost because the Son of God is dying! Was he really the Son of God? There is renewed solitude for Jesus as he goes on. He has no more disciples. They had not understood anything. This is new proof of the failure of his presence on earth.

What will he leave behind? A group of the faithful that denies him and other faithful ones who betray him? The distance is not so very great from denial to betrayal, and Jesus knows it. During the last supper, an incredible scene is painted for us, as all the disciples feel capable of betrayal. When Jesus says, "One of you will betray me," they are deeply saddened and *each one* asks him, "Is it me Lord?" This situation is unheard of. Of these disciples, the twelve chosen to be the nucleus of the Church, the first emissaries sent to proclaim the Good News, not one of them feels sure of himself, and neither John nor Peter hesitates to speak of it. On the one hand, they completely trust what Jesus is saying, not doubting that one of them will betray him, and on the other each one of them *feels capable* of betrayal. Yet, they love him—all of them do, even Judas. We are not told that Jesus reassured those who doubted themselves in this way. However, he did confirm that someone would betray him when he said, "One who dips bread into the bowl with me . . ." My companion. He only answers Judas. Perhaps we can hear a little difference in the question of some. The other apostles say, "Is it me, Lord?" thereby recognizing that Jesus is the Lord, come from the Father. Judas calls him *Rabbi.* Judas is not as certain of this divine lineage.

John recounts the scene in a different way. Peter has John ask who will betray Jesus (the apostles continue to be unsure of themselves). Jesus gives the piece of bread he had dipped—with a singular allusion to Communion—to Judas, designating him through an ambiguous symbol. Then, without any anger or condemnation, he says to Judas, "What you are about to do, do quickly." At the beginning of the account, John tells us that Jesus *"was troubled in spirit"* when it becomes known to him that one of his faithful will betray him. Here again, we see the suffering of the one who is completely Love, who loved Judas and chose him. It seems vain in my view to ask whether Jesus (divinely) knew that he was calling a traitor to be an apostle. Judas also had good qualities. Judas was not a traitor from the beginning. This is the fulfillment of Scripture. One of them, one of those who proclaimed the Good News, will betray him. Jesus is infinitely sad, and after he has told them that he must soon suffer and die, there is still uncertainty, even after Judas leaves. Jesus knows he cannot trust these men: "Tonight, I will be a stumbling block *for all of you.*" The disciples are not wrong in doubting themselves! The one who protests and proclaims his faithfulness is the one who will deny him the most explicitly!

The Kiss

How disgusted the authors of the Gospels must have been when they emphasized that Jesus was betrayed by *a kiss*! The brotherly kiss becomes a sign of being put to death . . . And what an abyss of sadness it must have been for Jesus to be kissed *thusly* and for that *reason!*

Once again, let us remember, Jesus is not a superman, not a stoic—quite the contrary, he has a deeper sensitivity than the average person. So these scenes that we have been reading—and in which the reaction of Jesus is not often told to us—must not be read as an adventure happening to a Son of God who is "well above" these denials and these betrayals . . . No, Jesus is the person who feels even more keenly than we do everything that a person could suffer: the betrayal of a friend, the abandonment of those closest to him. One word, incidentally, indicates this: he was troubled in his *spirit*—which is precisely what connects him to the Father and which was most central and most essential in him. It was "shaken" or "troubled" or "stirred." How forceful this simple statement is and how great the misery inflicted on Jesus.

The Refusal

As we make our way through these texts relating the suffering of the Son of Man, we must give some space to the negative reactions that he encountered from all. First, we have the many stories recounting how Jesus is rejected by the very same people he heals or saves and by those who witness a miracle (Matt 8:28–34). "Then the whole town went out to meet Jesus. And when they saw him, they pleaded with him to leave their region." Of course, this resulted from their having lost their herd of pigs! That is not the reason, however; if that had been the case, the text would have said that the owners were furious. No, they came to plead with Jesus to leave because they were faced with a power so great they could not bear it. Those who became his disciples felt the same way. After the miraculous catch of fish, Simon Peter threw himself at the feet of Jesus and said, "'Go away from me' . . . For terror had seized him and all those who were with him" (Luke 5:9).[9] Many people certainly came to Jesus in order to be healed, but so many times we also see the fear of being confronted by a reality that is infinitely beyond us. We might compare this to the requests for a miracle for the sake of a miracle, as long as that miracle is nothing more than a fairground attraction, an entertaining experience of the extraordinary. This was the case with Herod: when Jesus is to appear before him, the latter is quite happy because, "from what he had heard about him, he hoped to see him perform some miracle" (Luke 23:8). A magician or a wizard—that is always interesting, but those who actually witnessed a miracle by Jesus were very much aware that another kind of power was involved; and they were afraid. This shows again the constant misunderstanding with which Jesus was confronted. This is a misunderstanding that will resist all the "pedagogical" forms that Jesus uses: parables, references to the Bible, "catechetical" teaching, direct declarations, great public speeches, and explanations following a miracle. Nothing will clear up the misunderstanding. It has persisted throughout the history of the church and continues today.

MOCKERY

One of the most despicable aspects of this fundamental incomprehension was mockery. Let us never forget that Jesus was an object of mockery and derision for people. Mockery stems from the fact that the man who does not understand anything about "the other" proclaims himself infinitely superior to him by ridiculing him.

When we are tempted to make fun of our neighbor, let us always remember the mockery to which Jesus was subjected and

9. Translation of Louis Segond.

let us not forget that the root of it is incomprehension. When Jesus is about to perform one of his greatest miracles, the raising of the daughter of Jairus, and declares, "She is asleep," people laughed at him rather than understanding the importance of reducing death to sleep (for it is true that for Jesus death is a sleep). The only solution is to send them away (Matt 9:24–25). This seems to me to be all the more important as Mark notes that those who were there were crying and wailing loudly . . . which means that their grief was only a show and a refusal to let God be God. Their tears are hypocritical and they are unable to hear the words, "Don't be afraid, just believe."

We see the same situation when Jesus has finished his important lesson on how to manage the goods of this world (in the parable of the shrewd manager)—the Pharisees sneered at Jesus. Of course, he had called into question all the proper rules of business; and it was clear that he did not know anything about the topic. The Pharisees sneered at this foolish teaching. For once, however, Jesus responds to the mockery: "You seek *to appear* just before men, but God knows your hearts. What is *highly valued* among men is detestable before God" (Luke 16:15).[10] This is a fundamental answer to the mockery that comes from "superiority." Jesus does not explicitly say what is "highly valued." It is not necessarily riches or power—it could also very well be what is "spiritual" (of which we are so fond!) and "having lofty thoughts"; or it could be morality, that is, the dignity we give ourselves when we do good!

So let us remember that it is indeed suffering for Jesus. This is not only the unpleasantness of being mocked but the suffering caused by incomprehension and unbelief. The mockery will become tragic when we come to the behavior of the soldiers and of those present at the crucifixion, the mockery of decking him out with the false badges of power: a scarlet robe, a crown, and a scepter. This mockery is actually addressed to God, for there is no power other than Caesar. Who is this little Jew compared to Caesar? This is deriding the lordship of him who did not declare

10. Translation of Louis Segond.

himself lord and Son of God but who knew it and who suffers from derision that is actually directed at the Father! It is also directed at *his people*! For Jesus is always bound to his people. At no point did he deny the chosen people—the attacks on the scribes and Pharisees have nothing to do with that; quite the contrary, we have seen how he suffered because the chosen people was like a flock of sheep without a shepherd.

Luke recounts another mocking scene during those tragic hours: the men who surrounded him covered his face, struck him, and challenged him to say who had done so. Earlier, they had been deriding his lordship based on the ignorance, the incomprehension, the stupidity of what the lordship of God can be—let us not forget that still today we encounter the same triumphant silliness about this lordship! Now, their derision was for the prophet, the seer, the man who worked miracles. They asked him to perform a little "conjuring trick." In reality, here again, the mockery came from stupidity and ignorance: They had not understood anything about the depth of these miracles, miracles that were the expression of love.

Later, at the most tragic moment, we will see mocking that is more closely related to temptation. Everywhere, Jesus is faced with this mockery: from the priests (Matt 27:41), from the Pharisees (Luke 16:14), from the soldiers, from people in general (Luke 22:63), and from the magistrates (23:35). It comes from everything that is "highly valued." The persistence of the mockery that Jesus faced has helped me understand a phrase to which I had not paid much attention: "Happy the man who does not sit in the seat of mockers" (Ps 1:1). I thought it was somewhat of an exaggeration to put the mockers on the same level—as this text does—as the wicked and sinners. The mockery leveled at Jesus reveals what a mocker really is: a fool who feels superior and derides what he does not understand.

Right from the start, Jesus has no illusions as to what is awaiting him and the welcome that will be given to his gospel. As he is moved with compassion for the crowd, he knows too that this crowd will not receive his apostles. When he sends them off on their mission, he has an astonishing twofold message for them: on the one hand, to heal, purify, and proclaim that the Kingdom of God is at hand (Matt 10:7–10); and, on the other, "I am sending you out like sheep among wolves. They will flog you. They will judge you because of me" (Matt 10:16–20). So he has no illusions regarding those who move him to pity. The more excellent your words and your works, the more you will be hated. Jesus knows very well that this will be true of him first of all. He is expecting no gratitude, no love, no trust. Beyond mockery, he is expecting hatred, a hatred that his apostles will experience first.

He knows in advance that the reception he will receive from men and their hatred will be exactly in proportion to his love—its inverted figure. Jesus is total love incarnate. He will thus provoke total hatred, which lives on today and takes on all kinds of forms— from torture to the hypocrisy of the church and of Christian powers, which, no matter what they do, never advance beyond the speech of the Grand Inquisitor in Dostoyevsky. The more his ministry develops and takes shape, the more his teaching is heard, and the more his miracles are certain, the more the judgment of the world and the harshness of its reaction become clear as well. Little by little, Jesus gives his disciples a teaching on his "failure" and on his death. "We are going up to Jerusalem and the Son of Man will be *betrayed* to the chief priests and the teachers of the law. They will *condemn him to death* and will *turn him over to the Gentiles* to be *mocked and flogged and crucified*" (Matt 20:17–20). These six pronouncements of his suffering are all important.

Of course, the assessment of a rationalist reader will be that Jesus never uttered these statements and that they were added after the fact. But what is extraordinary about these statements? Is Jesus not capable of drawing the correct lesson from his three-year ministry and from the successive failures he has experienced? Does he not, from a human point of view, know that the political and religious leaders of the people are hostile to him? He has often provoked them. The Roman authorities are also inevitably hostile because he appears to be an agitator. Henceforth, he can expect arrest and condemnation. It is not necessary to see a divine revelation or a word from the Holy Spirit. We might also remember that the prophets' words were often simply the correct interpretation of the political or social situation. They draw the spiritual conclusion and announce God's answer.

THE WAY OF THE SON OF MAN

It is also true, however, that for the fulfillment of the work that was undertaken, "the Son of Man must suffer many things and be rejected and put to death"(Mark 8:31); and as a corollary, "Blessed are those who are persecuted because of righteousness, for theirs is the kingdom of heaven." These two declarations must be read in parallel. On the one hand, Jesus "must"—it was necessary. Why? It was necessary simply because Jesus came to share the human condition completely and the human condition consists of suffering and misunderstanding. To be as close as it is possible to any and all men, the Son of Man therefore has to suffer. The height of this obedience is the willingness to die. At the same time, he makes the statements on those who are "blessed" from the very beginning of his ministry. His own suffering and the persecution that he experienced come as a guarantee to ensure this blessedness. Jesus suffered to bring the righteousness that becomes the justification of anyone before God through the death of his Son. All those who are persecuted for righteousness' sake can now embrace this certainty: they are joining Jesus, just as Jesus joins any person who suffers. When Jesus announces his death, he is only applying to himself what he has already proclaimed to all in this beatitude. Human "logic" thus leads to this terrible declaration. He knows that it will bring the final end to his work but also that it will give him an unquestionable authenticity. He was the man who shared the suffering of all people. He did not merely "preach" righteousness, love, and truth. He is neither a philosopher nor a guru; he came as a witness that non-power is the only true way for humanity. He lives the opposite of what the texts in Genesis tell us about people and their separation, and he goes to the extreme—final suffering and death. Henceforth, one can no longer argue about any of his testimonies.

TRUE OR FALSE WORDS OF JESUS

This is why, for instance, the meticulous search for the "true" words of Jesus is wholly futile, for one could only discern them through rational-critical methods that are opposed to the existential seal that the condemnation and death of Jesus give to these words. The only problem is this: Once his death is indisputable and condemnation has been pronounced on him, are the reported sayings, parables, exhortations, and admonitions compatible with this? Do they or do they not herald this future? To the extent that this coherence is found in the gospel records, it is futile to argue about this or that story, this or that miracle. The life of Jesus as recounted in the Gospels is the life of the suffering servant. Everything said about it is true.

DEATH

Finally, we may need to ask ourselves one more question. Actually, it is always the same question. Jesus, the Son of God, announces his condemnation and his death. Yes, but he was the Son of God. And in many stories he also announces his resurrection. We immediately think that since he knew that he would vanquish death and that this was the will of his Father, it must have been much easier for him to accept suffering and death. Yet, to have foreseen that it would be so does not change anything of the horror of his suffering, and declaring that this is the will of God does not change the reality of physical pain or the reality that death is the last enemy to be vanquished. It is the anti-god, and Jesus himself will be delivered to this anti-god!

There is no consolation in the prediction or even the certainty of the ultimate victory. Knowing that this is indeed the will of God does not make anything easy.

God's Will

Why was this necessary? Jesus is a man, and as such, he cannot avoid asking the question posed by countless readers (myself included) who are so often scandalized by this "must." Would God not have some other means? He who came in the person of Jesus accepted being the ultimate means of God. Precisely in order to be the means—with no cheating—his suffering had to be absolutely horrific suffering and his death had to be the most tragic, not only because of the physical suffering but because of the knowledge of death that Jesus possessed! He knew much more of death than any person, and this is why it was so much more terrible for him than for anyone else.

The Cry

This leads us to the last expression of the boundless suffering of Jesus, this cry: "My God, my God, why have you forsaken me?" Could the Son of Man actually go beyond that? People who feel or believe that they are abandoned by God only experiences a pale reflection of what Jesus experienced in this unthinkable dereliction. It is unthinkable. How can God die? How can the Father—who is Love—sacrifice his Son? How can Jesus, the Son of the Father, be abandoned and no longer call him "Father" and instead address him as "God," like any person abandoned by God? How is all this possible when Jesus proclaimed that "I and the Father are one"? It is unthinkable and incomprehensible even for Jesus the man, who could not help but feel abandoned because he dies without any succor. Furthermore, he feels "cursed," because he knows the Torah perfectly and knows that whoever "hangs on the tree" is cursed.

As the relationship between God and God is broken, a rift is brought about within God Himself—unthinkable! Jesus also knows the human suffering of one who concretely sees the failure of his work. He attempted to give the Jews a new and true interpretation of the law; he did not break the foundation of the Torah but going beyond legalism and external use, attempted to give it new life, power and depth, going beyond the doctors of the law in situating the Torah in the existential aspect of life. The chosen people really had to be the chosen people. Everything now ends here with the greatest failure in history. The one who loved his people so much is rejected; the one who labored for the God of Abraham is rejected. What more terrible suffering could there possibly be?

The Son of Man is not privy to the secret plans of the Father; he says so himself when he declares that he does not know the hour of the end of time—only the Father knows. That is normal. Because he is a man, he does not know everything about God but "only that which the Father has revealed to me." As Jesus, he is not the Lord omnipotent, but he thanks the Father for "giving" him these men and can account for them: "I did not lose any of those that you gave me."[11] To the suffering of the Son of God, we must therefore add the human suffering arising from a work into which he had poured all his courage and hope.

The reader will no doubt have noticed that this is the initial phrase of Psalm 22. Some will therefore conclude that on the cross, Jesus prayed the psalm that ends in a declaration of faith and in absolute certainty. Yes, that is quite correct—nevertheless, *that particular phrase* was the one that Jesus cried out and not any other phrase from the psalm! It is precisely after uttering this phrase that Jesus can declare, "It is finished." This means, first of all, that he fulfilled the whole law—he was indeed the suffering servant, the one who was abandoned by God, the one who was cursed, the innocent one, as many texts of the Torah proclaim; but it also means that he went as far into suffering as can possibly be conceived. He finished bearing all the suffering that is humanly conceivable, and

---

11. Many Christian readers will be scandalized at this presentation of the humanity of Jesus. They should meditate on the words of the apostle Paul: "When it says that 'everything' has been put under him, it is clear that this does not include God himself, who put everything under Christ. When he has done this, then the Son himself will be made subject to him who put everything under him so that God may be all in all" (1 Cor 15:27–29).

no person can suffer more than what God himself suffered in Jesus Christ.

A Simple Reading of the Gospels

We have now covered the cycle of the suffering of Jesus. I have tried to do so without emphasizing the emotion that we may feel and without romanticizing that suffering. In any case, I certainly did not try to explain the "psychology" of Jesus. This research on his suffering is not based on an analysis of the character of Jesus. I simply contented myself with reading the Gospels. I do not believe I added anything to them. The result only arrests us when we start putting the texts together. Sometimes, there is only a simple word intimating the suffering. As one puts these statements together, ones that are in no way formulaic, one is struck by their number and their diversity.

And the Fear of Tomorrow?

Nevertheless, I think one remark must be added. I said that Jesus experienced all the suffering of men. Actually, he did not. He did not know the sickness that afflicts modern humanity, one of the most common diseases of developed nations. This is the fear of tomorrow, the fear of "lacking" (lacking food, lacking a clean natural environment, lacking employment . . .), the worry—often completely at odds with the facts—the anxiety that drives people to tranquilizers and anti-anxiety drugs. Jesus did not experience any of that. The anguish at Gethsemane is not that kind of anxiety. Anguish is the great mover of existential questioning, and he was familiar with that. But the rest—all the mental troubles—those he did not know. All the suffering he experienced came from without: the insults, the mockery, the blows, the fatigue . . . All of that was very real and was inflicted on him by people or circumstances. But the imaginary fears and the suffering that come from the depths of our being today, those he did not know. How can I be sure of this? Simply by rereading his own advice: "Therefore I tell you, do not worry about your life, what you will eat or drink; or about your body, what you will wear . . . Who of you by worrying can add a single hour to his life? So do not worry! Your heavenly Father knows that you need these things . . . Therefore do not worry about tomorrow, for tomorrow will worry about itself. Each day has enough trouble of its own" [Matt 6:25–33]. Jesus says what he lives. Just as he lives what he says.

Thus, Jesus did not worry about tomorrow; he was not anxious. In regard to what is going to happen, he trusts and commends everything to the Father. That seems to me to show the seriousness of our situation today, for this is a most radical condemnation. Modern people are assuredly the most extensively protected by insurance, by attempts at controlling the future and by safety and medicine and guarantees of all sorts—yet they seem to be the most anxious people who have ever existed. They are afraid. Jesus, however, says that he is not afraid and says why. With the simplicity of truth, he tells us how it is possible to live outside this anxiety. Yet, that is precisely what modern people *do not want* or more *cannot* bear to hear any longer. They cannot allow tomorrow to retain its secrets, cannot bear to have no hold upon it. Everything must belong to them. They want to have everything. They covet security and the future. And to that extent, they are dying of anxiety. They want to be master in all things and therefore cannot bear to allow the smallest reality to lie beyond their grasp! Jesus never claimed to predict anything or insure anything and was therefore quiet and at peace.

Was it easy for Jesus? Certainly not! Jesus was fully human, and as such, he may also have wanted to dominate the future.[12] Here we are approaching temptation, but he tells us how to live in peace. Because he himself was reconciled to the Father and because he reconciles us, he also offers us reconciliation to ourselves.

---

12. The refusal of Jesus to "fabricate" his tomorrow seems to me very important to deflate the conceit of certain theologians who speak of a "strategy of Jesus" discovered in the gospel. NO, Jesus was neither a strategist nor a tactician.

We will therefore be without worry. We are now faced with the difficulty we encounter when salvation by grace is proclaimed to us. We want to be *sure* of this salvation and then "accomplish" it by ourselves. If I do this . . . I can be assured of salvation. This is precisely the great temptation: It requires nothing less than *escaping* from the free will of God! It is binding God! It is infinitely more difficult for us *to believe* in this salvation by grace—that is, to trust in the good will of God. For we are so used to taking possession by ourselves—never trusting anyone—to accomplishing all sorts of feats to control our future and our salvation by ourselves.[13] Jesus did not know this scourge that afflicts modern people, and this seems to me the most radical condemnation that could be made of a civilization that has devised a form of suffering that Jesus did not know—he who bore all human suffering and who for each instance of suffering stands by each person in that pain.

13. This conceit is not new. During the thirteenth century in France, people used to say, "The king holds his power from no one—except God and himself." Philippe the Fair changed the traditional formulation and proclaimed, "The King of France holds his power from no one—except his sword and himself"!

PART TWO

The Temptations of Jesus

He Was Tempted in All Things

"He has been tempted in every way, just as we are—yet he did not sin" (Heb 4:15). Earlier, the author said, "Because he himself suffered when he was tempted, he is able to help those who are being tempted" (Heb 2:18). In those two essential passages, we note, firstly, the link between suffering and temptation—which we have already discussed—and, secondly, the phrase "in all things": there is thus no human temptation that Jesus did not know. It is not only, as the Epistle to the Hebrews says, that he is for this reason able to help us—because he is acquainted with *everything* that we go through as far as temptation is concerned—but this also bears witness to the fact that he was *fully* human. For each one is tempted in such and such a way and knows various and diverse temptations, but only he knew *all* temptations. Nevertheless, we will attempt to avoid giving free rein to our imagination and write a novel or make a film of Jesus as object-subject; instead, we shall confine ourselves to what the Gospels tell us as they present the temptations of Jesus. We must not go beyond that. We shall moreover see that it is quite enough!

Do we need to say that it is not God, his Father, who tempts him and makes him go through the storm of temptation? There is no temptation that is not human. This is also true for Jesus. In other words, because he is fully human, there is in him everything that could become a source of sin; he has in him the roots of temptation but will never give in to it. He knows what we do not—how to win out over temptation. In all its forms, this temptation has only one objective: to make the man Jesus usurp the place of God, renewing the action of Adam, who wanted to be like God. That is all there is to it—but it is also everything. This is what Paul means in the famous text to the Philippians: "He did not consider equality with God something to be grasped." He knew this ultimate temptation. The one who leads him there is always the same enemy: the devil. We discussed Shâtan earlier, and what I have to say about *Diabolos* is similar. It is not *one* character or power but the symbolic representation of a diverse and multifaceted reality. The *Dia-bolos* is the one who separates, divides, and shatters unity. Hence, whenever there is a rupture, a rift, a divorce among people, we see the devil. We humans are quite sufficient to be the devil. As far as Jesus is concerned, there is also a rift between him and other men as well as a corresponding rift between him and the Father. The devil attempts by all means—including the good—to bring about a rift between the Father and the Son, that is, within God himself! This would be the ultimate triumph for the devil.

To close this short introduction, I would like to quote a passage from Antoinette Butte. What she has to say is particularly well realized in the life of Jesus:

> It is through Prayer that you will know temptation
> . . . Through prayer . . . temptation. Temptation is in the
> hand of God as man's freedom and dignity are. Without temptation there is no freedom. From temptation,
> attempt, *peirasmos,* comes experience. Man was born
> to freedom on the day of choice—the apple in the Garden of Eden. It is precisely here that we find the scene
> of real struggle, the struggle of prayer. Wherever man
> prays, there is the place where Satan attacks. This is the

dangerous condition of the Christian and of the Church, which is attacked more than anything else.[1]

THE DIMENSIONS OF TEMPTATION

Here, I will venture into an interpretation of the text that might surprise or scandalize the reader. It seems to me that right from the start of his ministry, Jesus posited the dimensions of his temptation when he gave his interpretation of the Torah and when he proposed a model for living that is unattainable. After affirming that not one iota—not one stroke of the pen—would disappear from the Torah and that all the commandments are equally important, he continues (in Matt 5:21–48) with these terrible words, of which we are always tempted to say "they are not for us": "You have heard . . . Do not murder . . . But I am telling you that all anger is murder. You have heard: Do not commit adultery. But I tell you that anyone who looks at a woman lustfully, has already commit adultery with her in his heart. You have learned 'an eye for an eye' but I tell you not to resist the wicked . . . You have learned: 'Love your neighbor and hate your enemies.' But I tell you: Love your enemies."[2] It has often been said the Jesus "spiritualized" the law, that he showed great freedom where it was concerned, to the point that he made it even more difficult to follow than all the prescriptions of the Pharisees. To be in the presence of this law is thus to be constantly tempted to break it. What Jesus says here concerns himself first of all. He announces to us how he is going to live, what his program for being will be. And thus he also tells us which temptations he himself will encounter in order to live out what he says—the truth of God his Father. Therefore, we can know that he experienced each one of the temptations he cites and that he overcame them.

1. In Communauté de Pomeyrol, *Le chant des bien aimés*.
2. [This is Ellul's paraphrase.]

The Three Temptations in the Desert

We must now start with the three temptations reported in Matthew 4:1–10, Mark 1:12–43 (accounts without any comment) and Luke 4:1–13. I have already written about these three temptations on several occasions, but how could we leave them aside when they first of all contain all the other later temptations and secondly are most relevant to our times.

The Desert

The first remark I would like to make—and which is essential— is that the Spirit leads Jesus into the desert (the Holy Spirit, says Luke). Mathew's affirmation is more serious: he is led into the desert to be tempted. The desert is the traditional place where "spirits" dwell, the place where the scapegoat is sent, and the place of trial par excellence. We have said that God does not tempt us or force us to undergo temptation. Sometimes, however, he sends us into temptation. Jesus was brought by the Spirit into the desert *in order* to be tempted by the devil there. Is Jesus aware of this "in order to"? It is unimportant; he goes where the spirit leads him. He subjects himself to the very conditions that will give rise to the trial: he fasts for forty days, which is reminiscent of the forty years Israel spent in the desert as well as Elijah's forty days. He is weakened by this first trial.

When the devil, the separator, comes to him, he is a weakened man who is not at the height of his powers. Is that important? Certainly. "God chose the weak things of the world to shame the strong." The devil is certainly strong. And if Jesus wins, it is not because he is in great "athletic" form or at the height of his powers. I can already hear the protests of some readers: "If Jesus wins?" But, if he is God, how could he not win? We certainly have a decisive question here; it is of the same order as the question about his death on the cross: because Jesus is God, he *could* not have *died*. Or some will say, "He knew that he would rise from the dead." Therefore, there is no "real" death. We must absolutely reject these statements. For if he is God, he did not fool us, did not pretend. Otherwise, his death and all of his life would have been a colossal fraud, a mockery. No, although he was God, he was as fully tempted as any person (but with what higher risk!), and he really did die in the horror of abandonment.

If Jesus wins, it is by the sheer grace of God and his complete responsibility. But Jesus could have lost. He could let himself go. He could have accepted such reasonable propositions. For let us remember that Jesus did not meet a character with wings and horns who began a dialogue with him! There is *no one* facing him . . . only himself. The questions and the suggestions that come to him are only coming from within. He is asking those questions of himself. They are so reasonable! And the moment is tragic. If Jesus wins and rejects the temptations, he wins *nothing but* a life of grief and toil, a life of renewed temptation all the way to the cross. And if he loses, if he obeys one of these reasonable propositions, he wins everything on earth . . . But then, God himself would have lost everything; this is because the final means chosen by God to show his love to all men would have been lost just like the previous ones! What a great risk there is in this bet, which is the opposite of the wager presented by the philosopher Blaise Pascal.

Bread

After a forty-day fast, Jesus is hungry! The simple thought that comes to him is inevitable: Why not transform the surrounding stones into bread? Why not perform a miracle? He will perform so many of them! And perhaps the question springs up in his mind: if I really am the son of God, it is possible. It would be some kind of proof that he could give himself. Thus far, there had only been legends from his childhood or an illusion at the time of his baptism . . . After all, why would Jesus not have needed additional certainty?[3] God has indeed sent me, and I am indeed his Son, the Messiah . . . These are not blasphemous questions since no one

3. See Dreyfus, *Did Jesus Know He was God?*

has ever been able to explain the co-existence of the "two natures." The issue is to prove that he is the Son of God by performing a miracle.[4] We will find this temptation throughout the Gospels, but it is usually men who are asking for the proof. Here, we begin with a question that contains all the subsequent questions. We are warned that whenever Jesus is faced with this question, it will be because the devil is speaking through one person or another. Yet, in itself, this proposition seems quite normal. A man is hungry; if he is able, why would he not find the bread needed to satisfy this basic need? We are forced to expand upon this and understand the proposition in its broadest sense. To satisfy a need—and here the need in question is *obvious*, that is, the most pressing hunger—calls into question the totality of modern civilization in its frenzy of production and consumption. Elsewhere, I have called this first temptation the economic temptation. The legitimization of all our activity, of all our inventions, and of all our production is that they satisfy our needs. As long as we can declare that if "we put a product on the market, it is because there is a corresponding need," anything can be justified. It is obvious that nuclear weapons correspond to a need from the military, that cars capable of 155 miles per hour satisfy a need for power, and that VCRs answer a need for constant entertainment . . . We can always invent a new need that did not previously exist but that will appear to be essential as soon as it is possible to satisfy it. Our economic life only exists to satisfy needs that themselves need to be created so that we can sell a new product. Once this need has been created, however, it becomes a *real* need and the absence of satisfaction is painful. It is not quite possible to separate natural needs from artificial ones, for artificial needs become natural ones. It is true that the morphine addict feels as strong a need for morphine as any person feels for

4. We are here in radical opposition to the Koran. All the miracles of Jesus recounted in the Koran (there are three of them, which are not recounted in the Gospels, and the miracles in the Gospels are not included in the Koran) are stupid miracles (for example, there is a table laden with food that Jesus brings down from heaven), their purpose is only to show his power and his domination. This is exactly the opposite of the meaning of the Gospel miracles.

food. The only difference is that the little newborn baby has a need for food and no need at all for morphine. The latter only becomes a need through the physiological manipulation caused by the use of morphine: it exists before the need. Certain needs only appear with the products that are required to create them.

I believe this brief story is all about our economic life. And of course, the devil had predicted the consequences: as soon as people were able to make these fantastic machines, they thought they were God. This characterizes us: we are really divine because we have transformed these materials, these substances, these natural elements, into elaborate products that can satisfy unimaginable—and truth be told—unknown needs. This particular judgment that "We are divine" is found in many places such as in cults of personality, the commemoration of important historical movements, the obscure writings used in Christian initiations, and the arcane texts laboratories produce, as well as the declaration so often heard these days: "I have *faith* in humanity." Of course, we should! Through the miracle of productivity, people have indeed *proven* that they are divine!

Faced with all this, Jesus refuses to perform this miracle of demonstration—even though he is hungry—and instead lays down a corner stone: "Man does not live by bread alone, but by every word that proceeds from the mouth of God." The hunger for bread is unquestionable. But hunger for the word of God—felt less obviously in the belly—is even more essential. He is not only saying, "I refuse to perform this miracle because I refuse *to prove* that I am the Son of God," but also "I—and all other men—hunger *first* for the word of God." This is not about denying hunger for food or the usefulness of providing bread to the starving, nor is it about producing what is really necessary for a person's life. It is about discovering that the word of the living God, the Being of all Beings, the Father, is even more indispensable to a human life *worthy of humans*—for in reality, the production of all our innumerable "goods" lowers people beneath that which is human . . . "'The days are coming,' declares the Sovereign Lord, 'when I will send a famine through the land—not a famine for food or a thirst for water, but a famine of hearing the words of the Lord. Men will stagger from sea to sea and wander from north to east searching for the word of the Lord, but they will not find it. In that day, the lovely young women and the strong young men will faint because of thirst. They who swear by the shame of Samaria or say "As surely as your god lives, O Dan" or "As surely as the god of Beersheba lives"—they will fall never to rise again!'" (Amos 8:11–14). Nourishment through the word of God is as fundamental for a person's whole being as bread is for the body.

A person is not only a body. If one keeps this body alive without feeding the whole being, then *everything* wastes away, even the body! This nourishment for the being can only come from being itself, only from the one who can say, "I am," for only he *is* without limits in time or space. He is the same today, yesterday, and forever. There is an exact correspondence between this being and the one to whom he gave being: "He becomes a living being." So when the spirit ceases to breathe upon him, this living being ceases to live, and can at best continue to exist, to be an existing being without meaning. When Jesus answers this temptation, he does not do so with piety or ideology but with the rigorous and universal expression of humanity found from its origins to the present and in all civilizations. Jesus makes his decision very explicit by using a simple parable: "What good will it be for someone to gain the whole world, yet forfeit his being? Or what can anyone give in exchange for their being?" (Matt 16:26).[5] This is the question that is asked in the first temptation.

How can we not think of contemporary society in which, thanks to technology, we have indeed "gained the world" but in which people have clearly lost their being? They have become empty of all being. They have become empty of all being and filled only with desire and entertainment.

5. In most translations this is rendered rather feebly with the word "soul." The reader is referred to the beautiful translation by the great Hellenist Hubert Pernot.

Power

The devil is not vanquished, for he immediately offers another proposition, a more subtle one, which will become a temptation. I will follow the order of temptations in the Gospel of Luke rather than the Gospel of Matthew because it seems to me more coherent. "The devil led him up to a high place [a very high mountain according to Matthew] and showed him in an instant *all* the kingdoms of the world. And he said to him: 'I will give you all their authority and splendor, for it has been given to me and I can give it to anyone I want to. So if you worship me, it will all be yours.' Jesus answered: 'It is written: "Worship the Lord your God and serve him only"'" (Luke 4:5–8). After the "economic" temptation, we now have the "political" temptation.

The first and very harsh pronouncement made by this text concerns precisely "the essence of the political." I have already made use of it in my studies of the State. The devil's declaration is very firm: political power in all the kingdoms, political glory, and political greatness all belong to the devil. This is of course very serious! Of necessity, this leads us to consider governments and powers in a different light. They are all emanations of Satan; they have all given allegiance to the devil; and they have all been received from the devil. This is true of the institution itself as well as the person who holds power at any particular time. The very famous saying that "Power corrupts, and absolute power corrupts absolutely" is both rooted in and explained by this text. Furthermore, this is not an unfathomable mystery: Who *wants* to wield power? Who *wants* to take advantage of political glory? Obviously, it is the person who is already possessed by a spirit of power. One "gets into politics" to satisfy one's will to power. The politician's discourse on "the public good" and his explicit devotion to the cause of humanity and so forth are all smoke screens about the reality of power itself and about all politicians. Our text is very harsh: those seeking political authority must not only be indwelt by the spirit of power but, what is more, must *worship* the one who can give this power—the devil, the tempter. Beyond him, such people must worship power itself. We can therefore say without hesitation that all those who have political power—even if they use it for good ("the devil also knows how to do good at times")—have received it through the devil and are, even if they are unaware of it, worshipers of *diabolos*. If this is the case with the proposal that the devil makes to Jesus, how could we believe that other men would be more unscathed than Jesus! But let us always remember that this thirst for power is only one particular expression of covetousness. Since Adam, it has been the keystone of all human maliciousness and voraciousness.

Power and Divisiveness

Yet one point must be made: Why is this temptation offered to Jesus by the *diabolos*? This will enlighten us as to the reality of the political! We have said that the *diabolos* is the one who divides. Is this not precisely what characterizes all politics whether it be from the left or the right, whether it be fascist or Marxist? Politics *divides*. It sets people against one other and classes against one other. It lays down theories and dogmas that create barriers, and the more politics claims to be "unifying," the more it divides. Without politics and political leaders, men would be able to agree and understand one other; but as soon as politics intervenes, they engage in all sorts of battles. So it is perfectly normal that the *diabolos* should offer power!

Power to Serve the Good

We are now faced with a difficulty: we have said that the devil is not a person, not a particular character, that he is instead a symbol of a human tendency. We have just described this tendency as the thirst for power, the spirit of power, and covetousness. How could all of this find any room in the person of Jesus? In other words, how can we believe that Jesus would have felt a thirst for power and the "urge" to conquer these kingdoms? How was this a real temptation for him? We might say that Jesus experiences it to the extent that he came to extend the Revelation of God in Israel and make it universal. How convenient it would have been, if he had had power over all the kingdoms so that he could spread the revealed truth everywhere and perhaps impose it upon them. He could have put political power at the service of the gospel and used it for good! Unfortunately, this notion hardly brings to mind the behavior of the church over the centuries. Obviously, people did not sufficiently meditate on these simple texts of the gospel! To the church of Constantine's time, the emperor should have been seen as the *diabolos* and not as the bearer of the sword to extend revealed truth!

All of this is quite true, yet it is not enough. The temptation that Jesus faces is more subtle and more radical. For the devil suggests that Jesus should accomplish right away exactly what the Father sent him to accomplish! For the Father sent the Son not only to proclaim the gospel to all but also to be a witness on earth and among men to the presence and power of God. He came to manifest the truth that God is higher than any human power—and not only from the height of his transcendence but also in the midst of humanity. Jesus came to be proclaimed "Lord" (Phil 2:9–11). In other words, the devil suggests that Jesus simply accomplish what God sent him to do! Yet, Jesus refuses. He refuses his own temptation to wield this universal power rapidly, to wield it himself by taking it.

Along with demonstrating the enormous impossibility of worshiping the devil, I believe that this refusal—the refusal of the temptation to take power when he knows he can only receive it from the Father—reminds us first of all that Jesus came to fulfill all of the law and all of revelation. He came first of all to be the suffering servant. He came first of all to be a man among men and not King and Lord over people on earth. If he had given in to the temptation, he would not have fulfilled all the prophecies and would have failed in the mission that God had entrusted to his Son.

Even more: there is the *right away*. To fulfill God's plan right away is in reality to take the place of God. And yet, this would have been so much more certain and convenient! It would have provided more certainty than finishing his ministry on an apparent failure, leaving the weight of truth to be carried by people who were not too capable and not too faithful. Uncertainty. Lord? But where was this lordship? How was it manifested? The devil's solution is so much more certain. At that moment, it is true that human freedom would have been taken away. So Jesus refuses political power and the rapid establishment of indisputable authority over all the earth.[6]

It Is Written

We must now call attention to the peculiarity of Jesus' response. First of all, let us note that he does not argue with the devil and does not tell him that his claim to be master over all the kingdoms of the earth is untrue. The true Master is God.

Indirectly, Jesus therefore confirms the devil's claim. For Jesus, it is apparently true that the devil distributes political power to whomever he wants. Jesus' answer is: "It is written . . ." During the first temptation, he had given the same answer and the same reference that "It is written," written in the Torah. Faced with the devil, Jesus uses no other weapon and no other argument than a reference to the Torah.[7] It is enough for him because it is the Word of God. Against the devil's promise, he replies with nothing but the revelation of God. He does not place himself on any moral ground but on the ground of obedience to the revelation already given, which is eternally given, which he finds in the Hebrew Bible,

6. Here again we see a complete difference with Islam, which precisely looks for power, acts through military conquest, and imposes its truth through this conquest. It is certain that if the devil had offered this power to Mohammed, he would have accepted it immediately!

7. This attitude on the part of Jesus must necessarily lead us to refuse the theory embraced by so many Christians since Marcion according to which the "Old" Testament must be more or less completely rejected!

and which he has come to fulfill. It is written: "I did not come to abolish but to fulfill" and "not one stroke or letter will pass away . . ." This weapon *suffices*. The devil does not insist. When faced with temptation, we will thus always find the true and sufficient answer in the Bible. Of course, we must be resolved to live out the answer.

Jesus refuses exactly what he came to earth to accomplish, his vocation, because the condition that is added is unacceptable in the face of the Word of God: "Worship the Lord your God and serve him only."[8] How necessary it is for us, in our time, to come back to this simple truth and to realize that we have so many other gods and that we serve so many other powers! "It is written." Everything is said.

Religion

We now reach the third temptation in ascending order (according to Luke, for it comes second in Matthew). This time, the devil changes tactics: since Jesus countered him with Torah, he will now use it too. The devil knows the text of this revelation. This should alert us. Our very use of the Bible belongs to the realm of temptation! It is not enough to know the Bible or to use it appropriately and find the text that would suit us. Why does Jesus not obey the text?

This is all the more strange because when the devil uses this text, he acknowledges implicitly that Jesus is the Son of God. "He will command concerning you." He only asks him to prove it, to attest to it with certainty. There is, however, some progress since the first instance of the devil's saying, "If you are the Son of God . . ." Of course, this is not the first example in the Gospels of "demons" recognizing in Jesus, the Messiah, the Son of God—but Jesus commands them to be quiet. Here, the temptation that he will often face is more severe and is founded on revelation.

8. Let us note in passing that all the "answers" Jesus gives are from the book of Deuteronomy.

How often have we used these texts in search of approval or justification or proof that we are indeed "Christians" and that our conduct conforms to the will of God? Here is precisely the first limit: *to use* the biblical text. That is, instead of listening and obeying, we try to justify *ourselves* by using the revealed text. Each time we use it in this way, we can be certain that we have fallen into temptation. Or when in a discussion, we use such and such a text to draw an argument from it. The Bible is neither a collection of recipes nor a collection of arguments. But there is something more serious: the devil uses the Bible to bring Jesus to the point of breaking away from his Father. Yet, these texts do exist and they are actually taken from this Bible. So what can we say? This is where the question of interpretation arises—after the question of our use of the Bible. The great rule is that no text, no verse, and no declaration can stand by itself. To separate a text from the totality of God's revelation will inevitably cause us to distort it. There is in fact a double separation that we must avoid: first of all, and this is a classic error, there is the separation of a verse or a sentence from its text, from its context. When we argue that it is possible to make the Bible prove "anything," we are perfectly correct if we separate a sentence from its context. The second separation is even more serious, however: it is to separate a text—which always refers to God or to the action of God—from the revelation of God and about God as a whole, as it is given in the *whole Bible*. In other words, we must study the text together with all of God's action in history, with his people Israel, and in Jesus Christ. Hence, there is a precise and rigorous limit to the interpretation of a text: each one can only be received and understood in relation to all the others and to all that we know about God through them (this is interpretation according to the analogy of faith).

Here, the devil takes one text—which is true, which is indeed from Scripture, and which is indeed about the Son of God—but he completely distorts its meaning by making what would be a miracle attesting God's love for his Messiah, for his Son, into some sort of demonstration-miracle, a miracle of the marvelous. This is precisely the kind of miracle that Jesus always refuses to perform because he would not accomplish the will of his Father at all if he fulfilled this prophecy for his own profit and were to appropriate it! That for which the devil asks is a miracle to prove that Jesus is actually the Son of God. In fact, however, Jesus came for the forgiveness of sinners and certainly not to "impress the crowd." In his work, he can only ask for faith ("Blessed are those who have not seen and yet believed"), and if the relationship to God the Father is a relationship of love and faith, the relationship to the Son is necessarily one, too. There are thus no proofs.[9] Even less will he grant what the devil wants since he is the antithesis of love. The devil wants a miracle of sheer power: to leap from the pinnacle of the Temple and not be injured. Jesus will always refuse to perform miracles in order to prove or convert or to show his power, *except* when his power is at the service of his love. The "miraculous" and the "marvelous" are totally excluded. Jesus would never have caused rose petals to rain on his friends! It is only when he must calm the terror of his disciples that he stills the storm or when a person needs to be delivered from his demons or a child from death. . . .

A Sign

Furthermore, everyone knows that, in New Testament Greek, the word *semeion* ("sign") is also used to refer to miracles. It is "a designated" sign. The miracle is never performed for its own sake. It is only a "signpost"—one should never look at the miracle but rather look in the direction to which it points and the reality which it seeks to manifest.[10] So in other words, the devil is asking Jesus to

9. This must, first of all, cause those who want to prove the revelation through science, history, philosophy, and so forth to think twice. These apologetic "proofs" are not any more acceptable than the proofs through miracles. Furthermore, it is a very important element in the relationship with the Jews: "Jesus is not the Messiah, and the proof of that is that the new heavens, etc., are not here." This opposite proof has no more value than the proof requested by the devil!

10. See the excellent book on Jesus' miracles written by Maillot, *Les miracles.*

do exactly the opposite of what he came to accomplish on earth on behalf of his Father. It is easy to understand that he breaks with the devil without providing any proof.

Tempting God

We must now focus on the response of Jesus, which is also taken from Scripture: "Do not put YHWH, your God, to the test." The response is essential because Jesus does not use this text to tell the devil, "You shall not tempt *me*," which would affirm himself to be the Son of God. Neither does he say to the devil, "You are tempting God." The meaning of the response is indeed as follows: "If I, Jesus ever did what you are asking me, then I would be tempting God. I would be tempting God to force him to manifest that I am his Son, to force him to fulfill the promises he has made. I would be testing him to know if I really could trust him and know if he really would fulfill his Word. I would be bringing some kind of challenge to God if I were to throw myself from the pinnacle of the Temple." If Job is right to argue with God and demand that "God should agree with him against himself," if indeed these words of struggle were an expression of faith on the part of Jesus, they would, on the contrary, actually be an expression of doubt precisely because he is the Son: because I am in doubt, I also want to see proof that these words are indeed uttered for me.

This should remind us that in any temptation experienced by humans, it is *first of all* God Himself who is tempted! (As in the Prologue to the book of Job.) This challenge that I feel in my flesh, my heart, and my thoughts as a reassessment of my whole being is a challenge to God. Each time a person experiences this reassessment, it is in the end—in the final analysis—on God that the temptation falls. For if humanity "is" not without God, God is not without humainty either.[11] It is not God who tempts people. It is people who tempt God. They do so in a thousand ways.

---

11. Vahanian, *La condition de Dieu.*

Man tempts God when he utters prayers that are not inspired by the Holy Spirit; when he doubts; when he addresses other intercessors than Jesus Christ; when he wants to "put God to the test" (as in the story of "the two flower beds" in the Komsomol of 1925); when he demands miraculous healing without questioning himself and without drawing any spiritual teaching from illness; when he expects God to do everything in a particular situation without bothering to search for every possible means; when he wants God to give Himself when *he* does not give himself; when he claims to bind God with his rites, his ceremonies, his liturgies, and the *opus operatum*. How can we actually qualify this human attitude? (Of course, in all these devotions or relationships to God, people *do not know* that they are tempting God!) These are in reality *religious* acts exactly like the miracle that the devil was suggesting to Jesus. It would be a religious act on the part of Jesus because it would be to fulfill the Word of God and at the same time show complete trust in God. If Jesus leapt from the pinnacle of the Temple with the certainty that he would not strike the ground, it would indeed be because he trusted his Father! What could be better? Could there be a more "religious" act? The religious character of this test, of this temptation, is confirmed by the fact that the devil conducted it atop the Temple—even the setting is a religious one! Religion is the supreme locus of the break with the God of Abraham and of Jesus.[12]

We have discussed the three fundamental temptations that people can know: the economic temptation, the political temptation, and the ideological-religious temptation. These are the three domains in which humainty wants to assert its power and ensure its autonomy and its greatness.

THE ASSAULT OF CONCRETE TEMPTATIONS

We have already said that Jesus encountered temptations throughout his whole life. We will begin by discussing what the Gospels

12. I have often showed that Judaism and Christianity are not religions.

tell us about these temptations. We will begin with the most common ones—those that concern us all and that we all suffer. We are
now broaching a topic that could prove shocking to many readers.

Riches

Would Jesus have known the temptation of money and riches, for
example? Considering the life he led, we immediately answer: No!
And yet . . . he was tempted "in all things." Would there not be
some signs of it? I can see at least one. Let us consider the parable
of the rich young man and let us look particularly at the ending:
"It is hard for a rich man to enter the kingdom of heaven. It is
easier for a camel to go through the eye of a needle than for a rich
man . . ." The disciples are very surprised and ask the question,
"Who can then be saved?" Is this not a strange question, for are
they themselves not poor men? This teaching should not concern
them! Jesus answers, "With man this is impossible." With all men.
All men are in one way or another rich. But what about Jesus? Is
he not a man? He was fully human like all of us. He must therefore
also have known the temptation of riches. Though he was poor
and so little concerned with material questions, we must believe
that he also sometimes could have desired riches.

   Finally, there is also Luke's simple and very ambiguous mention of women who were following Jesus and who "were helping
to support him out of their own means" (Luke 8:3). These were
Susanna and Mary called Magdalene (who assuredly was rich because she had been a prostitute—remember the "perfume of great
price"). When we use the word "prostitute," we immediately think
of the poor women who are on the streets. In this part of the em-
pire, however, the prostitutes were often "high-class" and earned
a lot of money. In other words, Jesus and the disciples lived to a
great extent from gifts given to them by wealthy people, especially
wealthy women. I am not saying that Jesus suffered the temptation
of "riches," but he did benefit from them, even if we find this to be
scandalous. Furthermore, he could not have evinced the violence

that he put into his attacks on money if he had not himself felt the force of Mammon. He would not have personalized money and he would not have presented the absolute incompatibility between God and money if he had not known its irresistible attraction. He did not seek to become rich; he did not do anything to that end. Yet, he was on his guard against that enemy . . . and that is already one aspect of the "economic temptation."

Sexuality

Let us now turn to the other great temptation that people have always faced: sexual temptation. We have usually dismissed the problem by presenting an asexual Jesus. We have so fervently insisted on the horrible character of sexual sin that it is unthinkable that Jesus could have experienced this temptation. It is correct that very few things in the gospel give us even the barest indication on the subject. We always insist on the "great temptations," the more radical ones. And yet, if we ventured to say that Jesus was tempted to use his omnipotence, no one would be shocked. If I say that Jesus could have been tempted sexually, however, it would cause a scandal. Of course, we must not simplify the situation, which is the case with all the authors who concluded from the story of Mary Magdalene that she was the mistress of Jesus. Nothing could lead us to suppose that, and neither is there any indication that the phrase "the beloved disciple" implied that Jesus was a homosexual. Yet, can we not say that Jesus, because he was tempted in all things, also knew sexual temptation but rejected it and devoted himself completely to his Father? I like Pierre Jean Ruff's study on Mary Magdalene.[13] He refers to her as "preferred associate" and "preferred collaborator." Further, "In relation to the whole life of Jesus, she is the symbol of love. Is it simply a mystical or Platonic love or a more tangible and incarnated love? Is not the importance of the relationship between Jesus and Mary Magdalene an argument in favor of his profound humanity . . . ?" After all, is it not to Mary

13. Ruff, "Marie-Madeleine."

Magdalene that Jesus reveals his resurrection before he did so to anyone else? One will object that she was not among the circle of the apostles. Granted, but did not the risen Christ make her the first evangelist, who was entrusted with bringing the ultimate good news of the resurrection to all the disciples?

In raising this question, I cannot refrain from saying a few words about the all-too famous Martin Scorsese film, which I consider mediocre and undeserving of the conflicts it created. In my opinion, both camps are wrong. What is this all about really? The dreams of the crucified Jesus, dreams of a life other than his own.

He dreams of a "normal" life. He wed Mary Magdalene, had children, is leading a peaceful life, and grows old quietly and uneventfully. After this long narrative of what was only a dream, however, the story returns to Christ hanging on the cross. Some traditional and very pious Christians were scandalized in the name of a very ethereal and perfect representation of Jesus the Son without any dreams or temptations, always faithful, and who could not have had any feelings except of obedience to the Father and of fulfillment of the law. This is a completely sanitized Jesus. But sanitized of what? Sanitized of all his humanity in fact. Such people remind us of those who were so strongly scandalized by Michelangelo's painting of Christ completely naked in the great fresco in the Sistine Chapel. Another painter had to add a rag to cover "the shameful parts." . . . Have they forgotten Jesus begging the Father to spare him this "bitter cup," Jesus trembling with horror as he faces death, Jesus asking the Father why he has been abandoned? For such Christians, Jesus is in reality a pure spirit, having nothing to do with the body. According to this view, he was indeed tempted . . . but only once by the devil. Afterward, he was rid of temptation! Do they understand that their calm painting could actually be a temptation? I will therefore reject this judgment made by the "orthodox" because it implies in reality the denial of the "two natures."

Yet, the other group, made up of those who defended the film, seems to me equally in error. Much has been said about the creative freedom of the artist (as long he does not say or depict idiotic things[14]) and some upheld the pure and simple humanity of Jesus, a Jesus who was quite simply a human being and who grew old peacefully. Mediocre, mediocre—and very much like the fabulous stories with which one has tried to explain that Jesus was never crucified—that there was a replacement, an illusion, a mistake . . . what we find in the Koran. Reality seems to me to be more profound: if Jesus knew the temptations of humanity (and it was necessary that he know them!), a human all-too human, why would he not at some point encounter this particular temptation: children, a family, tranquility . . . But there is not a trace of that in the Gospels. It is simply a supposition. If it ever happened, this mediocrity must have been quite fleeting! In my opinion, there could only have been a possible love for Mary Magdalene, immediately swept aside so that he could devote himself exclusively to the work that God had entrusted to him.

The Son of God

We are now approaching the domain of the constant temptation that Jesus faced, coming from everyone, either because of love and gratefulness, or because of mockery and wickedness. This temptation was all the greater and all the more central because it corresponds to the reality of what he is. Paul evoked this temptation clearly in the famous text in Philippians: he did not consider equality "with God" as something to be grasped. This temptation exactly reproduces the temptation of Adam when the serpent promised him that he and Eve would be "like gods." How do we know that this was a temptation for Jesus? Simply by the liveliness of his answers each time the question is broached!

Let us remember what we have already said. A man runs to him and throws himself at his feet and exclaims, "Good Master," and Jesus answers immediately, "Why do you call me good? God

14. There must be some kind of coherence after all between the chosen theme and artistic creation. Yet, there is *no* coherence between the Gospels *as a whole* and this film—which, moreover, is no work of art.

alone is good." He refuses to allow anyone to attribute to him what belongs to God alone. He refuses to enter into any competition, even to allow a hint of division. This clarity and this firm reference to "God alone" shows indeed that it was possible to call him Good Master, but in doing so, man does not know what he is doing; and Jesus immediately senses an impingement on the sovereignty of the Father. God is the unique one. He will often repeat it. Breaking the unicity of God is out of the question.

Yet, the interrogation nags at him. We know how careful Jesus is not to declare himself the Son of God. He only gave himself the name "Son of Man." Undoubtedly, in the Gospel of John, he declares that he is the Son of the Father. "The Jews tried all the harder to kill him [for] he was even calling God his own Father, making himself equal with God" [John 5:18]. Jesus answers this on two levels: "The Son *can do nothing* by himself, he can only do what he sees his Father doing, because whatever the Father does, the Son also does" (John 5:19). He subordinates himself in a radical way. The other response is ironic: the Jews want to stone him (John 10:33) "for blasphemy, because you, a mere man, claim to be God." Jesus replies, "Is it not written in your law 'I have said you are gods.' If he called them 'gods' *to whom the word of God came*— and the Scripture cannot be broken—what about the one whom the Father set apart as his very own and sent into the world? Why then do you accuse me of blasphemy because I said, 'I am God's Son'?" At that point, in other words, Jesus does not claim to be the Son of God any more than all those who have heard the Word of God! And those who attack him and respect the law should understand his "lineage." He is the bearer of the Word of God, but he is so to such an extreme and complete extent that this word has been incarnated in him. Once more, as he submits to the Father, it is from the word of God that he draws everything that he is: this is why he refuses to answer the question by affirming that he is the Son of God!

Before Caiaphas:[15] "*You* say so. But in the future you will see the Son of Man [of Man!] sitting at the right hand of the power of God."[16] The new Adam defeated the snare and did not usurp anything of God's glory. The temptation had to come from everyone, in multiple circumstances, yet it was compatible with the roots of covetousness-power, which—because he was a man—must have existed in him but which he knew how to uproot.

There is a temptation to respond to the desire of the crowd, and this came back again and again: "Everyone is looking for you," as Simon and his friends come and tell him triumphantly. Jesus answers, "Let us go somewhere else" (Mark 1:37). "When Jesus saw the crowd around him, he gave orders to cross to the other side of the lake," and it is at that glorious moment that he chose to teach that "The Son of Man has no place to lay his head" (Matt 8:18). If we read the texts carefully, we see that Jesus only accepts the crowd, that is, a great number of people, if there are sick or poor people among them. He flees as soon as a crowd comes out of *curiosity* (to watch him perform miracles) or if the crowd wishes to glorify him. He flees when they announce that "They are looking for you to make you king" (John 6:15). In other words, he absolutely refuses the temptation of notoriety, prestige, success, and glory given by the crowd. His renown spread more and more, and people came in crowds to listen to him . . . and he withdrew into the desert to pray. Perhaps he did so in order to overcome this temptation. If he came today, Jesus would inevitably refuse to make use of the media.

As for the crowd that acclaims him at his entry into Jerusalem, he has so few illusions about them that he himself *parodies* kingship!

---

15. This is Ellul's translation.

16. Furthermore, this text presents a problem: in Mark, Jesus answers Caiaphas's question with "I am" or "It is I." It is curious that Mark, who is considered older than Matthew, should contain this affirmation, whereas Matthew holds back a little, which conforms more to the attitude of Jesus during his ministry.

He has a little donkey colt brought instead of a war horse;[17] he makes do with palm branches picked in the field instead of a crown of laurels; and in the face of the joy of the crowd . . . he weeps (Luke 19:34–41). He has no illusion about the value of this glory and this renown: he knows that it will lead him straight to death.

The Self-Affirmation of Jesus

Along the lines of the temptation of glorification, we always encounter the question of self-affirmation. It is undoubtedly clear that Jesus always proclaimed that he was the Son of Man and never the Son of God—which is no proof that he was not—but rather proof that he rejected the temptation. Other situations are more subtle, as when he is acclaimed as the son of David. He does not himself choose that title although he does not reject it either (Matt 22:41–46). Thus, he escapes the question as well as the temptation to proclaim himself by responding skillfully. When the Pharisees rebuke him for not silencing the crowd that welcomes him on Palm Sunday and calls him that, he says, "Have you never read, 'From the lips of children and infants you have ordained praise'?" (Matt 21:16). A little later, he dismisses the question, as he often does, by asking his adversaries an unanswerable question: "You say that the Christ is supposed to be a descendant of David, how is it then that David, inspired by the Holy Spirit, calls him 'Lord' when he says: 'the Lord said to my Lord' . . . If David calls him Lord, how could he be his son?" (Matt 22:41–46). What Jesus knows in the deepest part of his being—for he cannot reject the fact that as the Messiah he *must* descend form David—he refuses to flaunt, proclaim, or declare to the crowd. Once more, he puts into practice what he himself advises: "Be careful not to practice your righteousness before man . . . When you pray, do not do it in public to be seen by men . . . When you give, do not let your left hand know what your

17. I know the hypothesis of certain historians who would like to see in his mount a war horse, but the formula "the colt of a donkey" denies the possibility!

right hand gives."[18] Jesus thus remains silent on what is the most essential. We are not saying that he wanted to hide his "divinity" and his "messianity," but he refused to yield to the temptation of exercising this other kind of domination over men, one that would necessarily have followed from these proclamations.

Judgment

We can find still other examples of his refusal to yield to the temptation of power. This will be the case in all the statements about judgment: "I did not come to judge." Very early on, in the parable of the wheat and the tares (Matt 13:24–30), he gives us the key to his refusal: one should not pull out the seeds before the harvest, for in judging too early, one also destroys the possibility for the wheat to ripen because it is pulled too soon. Hence, do not judge, do not hasten to condemn such and such a trend, or such and such an act in a person. There are possibilities for change within them, there is a future—still a secret to you—that you will destroy if you judge right now. I would add that we can perceive and "judge" a particular act; what is serious is to infer from that—*which we always do*—a judgment on the person. "He has stolen; therefore, he is a thief." This is the step we should never take. Only God can judge the person, we should only—and even here let us be careful—judge an act. In my opinion, a Christian is not even to judge an act or to forgive; rather, he should help the other out of a difficult situation and be the helper that might enable him not to repeat this act. The non-Christian, the judge within a legal system for example, can and sometimes must judge and condemn such an act. He should not go beyond that, however, whatever repetition may have occurred. The Christian must be there to rehabilitate the one who has (legitimately) been condemned by society for *one* action. He must restore the person's brokenness and give back human dignity.

Thus, Jesus refuses to judge even in insignificant cases. When a man trusted Jesus' sense of justice and came to ask him to

---

18. This is Ellul's translation of Matt 6:1–6.

arbitrate a dispute with his brother over an inheritance, he refuses by saying, "Who appointed me a judge or an arbiter between you?" Jesus is not an administrator of civil justice! This is essential in order not to confuse God's righteousness—fulfilled in Jesus—with legal justice. There is nothing legal in the work, life, teaching, or death of Jesus.[19] But if he refuses to be the judge and to affirm this sovereign power, he gives the plaintiff and the others present a fundamental piece of advice: "Be on guard against all kinds of greed." This is actually enough, for if the plaintiff watches out for greed, he will not show himself to be demanding and argumentative in sharing, will easily accept what the other requests, will not assert his "rights," and so the wealth will be shared without difficulty and there will be no lawsuit.

In the same way, Jesus refuses to judge and punish in circumstances that are infinitely more serious, as we see in the story reported by Luke of the judgment against a Samaritan village that had refused to welcome them (Luke 9:51–56). The disciples are furious and want to punish these hostile and inhospitable people and ask Jesus, "Do you want us to call fire down from heaven to destroy them?" (They do not doubt that it would be possible for them to do that, but they ask the Master for permission.) Jesus is extremely violent in his response: "You do not know what spirit is driving you!" You do not know but think yourselves very strong because you believe that you can command fire from heaven! In reality, you are ignorant spiritually and in matters of faith. You have not even understood why the Son of Man came! And what spirit? Once more the spirit of power, of vengeance, and of punishment! Is that what the Son of Man came to do? Is that what you have understood? And when there must be judgment after all, Jesus commends it all into the hands of the Father, who alone is the Judge (Luke 10:12—11:32–33)! Even the adversity that he announces is not a curse but a *prophecy* . . . He refuses to judge and condemn: such is the one to whom God finally commends the

---

19. This is true despite a number of studies I have seen that claim that in the Gospels, and especially in John, there are numerous legal allusions or a legal "framework"!

ultimate judgment, precisely because he overcame the temptation to judge and to manifest his power through condemnation.

Self-Justification

From this fundamental temptation to declare himself the Son of God on his own authority comes a wide array of other temptations. A whole series of specific temptations then appears only through the teaching of Jesus and explains why he will not do one thing or another. If he feels the need to say so, it is because he strengthens himself by attesting that he is right. First, there is the temptation to justify himself during the trial before Pilate. While he has still answered, "You say so," to the question, "Are you the King of the Jews?" Pilate asks him to justify himself concerning the accusations brought against him. Can you not hear how many accusations they are making against you? Jesus does not answer, however. He has no need to declare himself just. He has no need to prove himself right. No one justifies him. No one but the Father. He expects this justification only from the Father. Precisely because he would have impinged on what can only be the work of the Father if he had *proven* his innocence.

In the same way, when he gives new scope and new meaning to the Torah, he is very careful not to act like a Master of the Torah. It always remains the word of God, and he does not in the least want to usurp it, transgress against it, or abolish it. He makes this very clear, manifesting his submission to the Father; he does not want to go beyond the law—when he healed the leper he said, "See that you don't tell anyone. But go, show yourself to the priest and offer the gift Moses commanded as a testimony to them" (Matt 8:1–4; so that this obedience to the law may be a testimony).The Son of the Father respects the will of the Father and does not give in to the temptation of offering a new law. All that follows from this will have to do with power. Will Jesus use the power that the Father has entrusted to him? The temptation stemming from the Spirit of power obviously joins the temptation stemming from covetousness. He places himself under the law that he gave to all his faithful: "Anyone who exalts himself will be humbled, and he who humbles himself will be exalted" (Luke 14:11). He does not want to exalt himself, does not want to act out of power and domination, never wants to compel, will not perform vain miracles, will never use this power "for nothing," and will never relate anything back to himself. Paul says it firmly: "God chose the weak things of the world to shame the strong. He has chosen the foolish things of the world to shame the wise, and the things that are not to nullify the things that *are*" (1 Cor 1:27–28). God chose: God's elect, his Messiah, had to be weak and foolish in the eyes of the world; And "those who are not . . ." Because Jesus plunges into death, he of course *is* no more.

Yet, as a "thing that is no more," he is raised from the dead. When this takes place, he negates the power of death and along with it, all the powers that claimed to rule the world. Why did God choose this? So that "no flesh might glorify itself before God." So that the glory might exclusively be given to God and so that no one could say that Jesus was a learned exegete of Scripture, a powerful prophet, an initiate of the highest magic[20] and so forth . . . All the actions of Jesus and his whole life constitute a finger pointing toward the Father only. As far as power is concerned, we come back to what we said about goodness: do not look at me but only at the Father. All of his prayer life always comes back to: "I praise you Father . . ." and "Not my will, but your will."

Power

The temptation to manifest his power can be seen throughout his life: So many times he refuses to "perform a miracle!" The Pharisees and Sadducees (in agreement for once!) approached Jesus and asked him to give them a sign (*semeion*: miracle) from heaven. Jesus answered them, "When evening comes you say, 'It will be fair

20. This is why it is absurd to try to link the teaching or the miracles of Jesus to some Egyptian initiation.

weather for the sky is red,' and in the morning, 'Today, it will be stormy for the sky is red and overcast.' You know how to interpret the appearance of the sky, but you cannot interpret the signs of the time." Thus, there are signs that the time has come for the revelation of God's love, but these pious men who know the Scriptures are incapable of discerning the signs: they want one more sign. They want a sign for themselves in particular.

Is this not often what we Christians also ask for? We pray to receive some proof, a special revelation, that would convince "me" decisively, when the Scriptures should be sufficient! There are enough signs there! Jesus continues: "'A wicked and adulterous generation looks for a miraculous sign, but none will be given it except the sign of Jonah.' Then Jesus left them and went away" (Matt 16:1–4).

Why does he accuse "this generation"? He does so *precisely* because it is asking him for a miracle and because these men are doing so to "test him." They want to see what he is capable of. He calls them "an adulterous generation" because their request is false and dishonest: if Jesus were to grant their request, they would not be any more convinced after the sign than they had been before.

They are making this apparently pious request (for a sign from heaven) in order to set a snare! How often do we also ask for something or declare pious intentions that are really lies. "Adulterous generation"—why? They are adulterous because they want to believe for other reasons, on the basis of another revelation than the one already provided by God. They want to refer to something else than the word of God! They want a visible sign rather than a declared word. This is why Jesus sends them back to this word: there will be no other miracle than the miracle of Jonah. You know that particular miracle—it is found in your Scriptures, which you study so well. And actually, you would not be any more likely to believe even if you were to see a "sign." The Word, the Promise, the Covenant should be enough for you to discern who Jesus really is, that is, the one who fulfills the promises, the one in whom the

Covenant is confirmed . . . and the one who will indeed accomplish the miracle of Jonah, which was only a prophecy of what is to come.

But Jesus knows very well that his resurrection will not convince them any more than Scripture itself! This is also something addressed to us: How many times have we heard someone say, "If a dead person were to rise, I would believe"? Yet, the testimony of the resurrection of Jesus must suffice to give us the fullness of faith. In the end, why is Jesus so harsh with these Pharisees and Sadducees? Precisely because they are tempting him. It was a temptation for him to show his power. When he refused to do so, he knew that their reaction would be to say, "So, he is not the Messiah; he has not been sent by God." This is a real temptation. In order to be what he truly is, however, Jesus must not prove anything in this way.

Non-Power

This temptation will recur tragically. Firstly, at the time of his arrest in Gethsemane, when a disciple wanted to defend his Master, Jesus said to him, "Put your sword back in its place, for all who draw the sword will die by the sword. Do you think I cannot call on my Father, and he will at once put at my disposal more than twelve legions of angels?" But how then would the Scriptures be fulfilled, for according to them it *must* be so (Matt 26:52–54). These words—whose meaning are in harmony with the whole way of life that Jesus chose—are extremely rich. They denote,[21] first of all, a fundamental choice—the choice of non-power—that goes much further than non-violence. Non-power is not powerlessness, but rather the decision made by the one who has and holds a certain power *not to use it*, not to exercise the power that he could unleash, and not *even* to use it in order to defend his life. There is no "self-defense" in the life of Jesus. Once more he puts into practice for

21. My apologies to readers who will find an idea here that I have developed elsewhere.

himself what he preached in the Sermon on the Mount: if someone strikes you on one cheek . . . All Christians are called to make the same choice. We are now faced with a decision that is even more difficult than the decision about riches. This temptation is the most immediate and the most elementary—to defend one's life. The answer of Jesus is the same in the case of the temptation from the devil: I must obey the Scriptures. Everything announced in the Scriptures must be fulfilled, and he must therefore accept to be taken to the slaughter (we are put to death every day . . .). If Jesus were to ask the Father to send these legions of angels, he would be throwing the temptation he faces back at the Father. This corresponds to what we said earlier: temptation is always temptation of God! Now, however, it is no longer the devil that tempts but one of his disciples who does so by his action. Hence, temptation can come from those who are closest to us, the most faithful, the very best friends. This is confirmed by the text; as soon as Jesus refused to fight, the disciples abandoned him and ran away!

As I said: Jesus refused this power. His word is firm: he is certain that, if he asked, the Father would defend him! There is no hesitation: the Father would not leave his Son defenseless. What then would be the point of the Incarnation? What then would be the point of teaching and testifying? The Father would rescue the Son, but the great plan of reconciliation between humanity and God would have failed: the Son would then have preferred his own life to the gift that will reconcile humanity and God. So at this tragic moment, everything can still be lost—God's plan can fail. Jesus chooses to follow the Scriptures. He does not even seem to refer to the will of the Father. He knows that will beforehand. Those who arrest him and those who will judge and condemn him are only small fry who are acting in accordance with the perfect decision of Jesus, who has triumphed over the temptation.[22]

---

22. This text gives a definite answer to the hypothesis according to which Jesus would have been the leader of a revolutionary movement against the Romans and that the sword is symbolic—as were the two earlier swords. This hypothesis allowed a pseudo-theologian to declare that these swords "proved" that they had a stock of weapons! If that is what Jesus was, then we must also

Self-Preservation

At this moment, Jesus certainly knew the double temptation of avoiding suffering and avoiding death. We all know this vital impulse—everyone tries to avoid suffering and death—except when it is mastered by a more powerful reason for being, by the love of truth (or unfortunately, sometimes by hatred and ideology). In all this, Jesus is like us. For him, however, the manifestation of this vital instinct is a temptation—just as it is for someone who refuses to risk his life to rescue a drowning person. This is exactly what the Gospels recount in the dialogue with Peter. Jesus has just said that he must go to Jerusalem and suffer and die. Right after giving the great proclamation ("You are the Christ, the Son of the living God"), Peter exclaims that it is not possible, that none of this will happen to you! He places this conviction under the sign of God (Matt 16:22): "This cannot be the will of God . . ." Peter is logical with respect to himself; the declarations of Jesus are not logical, however: first, he congratulates Peter and declares that he is inspired by the Spirit of God when he proclaims him the Christ, the Son of God. And then Jesus announces that he is going to Jerusalem to *suffer* and *die*. For Peter (and for us!), this is obviously incompatible as well as contradictory. The violent reply of Jesus is extraordinary: "Get behind me, Satan! You are a stumbling block to me." Peter speaks like Satan: "Since you are the Son of God, what you are saying cannot happen to you!" Satan is always the one who drives us away from God and from God's will.

The important term here is "stumbling block"; the stumbling block is the snare. "You are setting a snare for me." In other words, Peter's protest is a snare for Jesus. But *would* it be a snare if it did not *also* correspond to some of what Jesus was thinking? It is a snare because for Jesus it is a temptation.

It is a real temptation, too. When Jesus declares that he must go to Jerusalem to suffer and die there, he is obeying a "must." His will certainly remains free, but if he followed it, God's plan would fail. He "must" do so to accomplish what the Father wants, but

_____

say that he was stupid and incompetent!

he has no desire to do so. The words of Peter are a snare for Jesus because they open up another possibility—one which would be so much easier—and one about which Jesus must inevitably have thought.

It is a temptation, and precisely because it is a temptation, Jesus replied so violently. It is the temptation not to suffer and die, which will return in Gethsemane. Just like any person would, Jesus dreads this ordeal. Perhaps the insistence of Jesus reflects this ordeal as he repeats at least three times, according to the Gospels, the necessity of suffering and dying. This fear is behind the meditative declaration that "I have come to bring fire on the earth, and how I wish it were already kindled! But I have a baptism to undergo, and how distressed I am until it is completed!" (Luke 12:49–50). If this is about the fire of the Holy Spirit, the baptism no doubt refers to his coming death . . . He expects it with anguish . . . He absolutely wants this difficult ordeal to be over, wants to have already walked through the valley of the shadow of death and be beyond it; then, the Holy Spirit would illuminate men. Right now, however, his whole ministry is within the perspective of this terrible ordeal; and as a man, he cannot but experience anguish in spite of all the certainty and in spite of his trust in the Father. He was tempted like us in all things, and as any person, he feared suffering and death.

This temptation is also present during the crucifixion—equally tragic but more impressive. The passersby insulted him and shook their heads saying, "You who destroy the temple and rebuild it in three days! Save yourself! If you are the Son of God, come down from the cross!" The priests, the scribes, and the elders mocked him, saying, "He saved others, and he cannot save himself! If he is the King of Israel, let him come down from the cross and we will believe in him!" We are again faced with the double edge of temptation: "Manifest your power," and "In this case we will believe in you." This is again the temptation to show, to prove, that he is the Son of God, the King of Israel. Jesus always refuses to offer proof, first of all because an "experimental" proof does not mean anything here and secondly, because their promise to *believe if he* offers proof is a lie.

This is the lie of humans because it is not true that they will believe that *faith* will reach them if the thing is *demonstrated* to them. There is a radical opposition between faith and seeing. If I provide proof, you can worship me as King of Israel, but you will not have understood anything or received anything; there will be no persuasion of the being, no *faith*. Precisely because he is coming in the name of the *invisible* Father—whose name cannot even be pronounced and whose Being is inconceivable—Jesus can only appeal to faith. And in order to "evoke" this faith, Jesus must resist this temptation. He could come down from the cross, could chose not to die. By doing so, however, he would destroy the possibility of faith in the God of Israel. Yet, he would be saving himself! He would cease to suffer, cease to agonize, could avoid the ultimate disaster for himself—not only the plunge into death but also the experience of being abandoned by God. At the time of this last choice, what does he receive from people? Mockery and insults (the robbers crucified with him insults, says Matthew)—this is the only help the Son of Man can receive. Faced with that, it would have been so simple, so easy, to ridicule them in return by accomplishing this miracle!

Your Will Be Done

A believer may also experience this temptation: to prove by a "gratuitous" miracle the power of the Lord . . . to put an end to doubts and mockery. Yes, but "not my will but yours be done." When asked for a miracle, we must remember, "Your will be done." We must nevertheless avoid a major misunderstanding here. Too often in Christianity, this phrase has been interpreted as a "maktoob" or an "insha'Allah," that is, a blind submission to the event that one presupposes to be God's will. Alas, this was too often the "consolation" offered to the afflicted and the suffering: "Bow down before the will of God." Yet, this is not at all the meaning of the request in the Lord's Prayer, nor is it the meaning of the decision that Jesus made in Gethsemane.

There are four movements to this prayer. First of all, we are asking to know God's will. This is neither obvious nor directly expressed in an event. What is God's eternal will and what is God's will in the here and now, in the circumstances in which I find myself? The second question is necessarily related to the first. For it is not enough to know the will of God. The second part of this request is: teach me to *love* this will. For it is only the love of this (known) will that will make life in God possible and that will make the third part possible: teach me to *do* this will. To know and to love and to fulfill—may Your will be done by *me*. But the prayer does not end there. If the will of God as it is discerned and loved should be contrary to my will, to my desire, my calculation, my interest, then help me to submit my will to your will so that this will might be done *in me*. There is no passivity in this prayer, no acceptance of what is happening, and no sloppiness, supposedly so that we can "let God act"!

Covetousness and Spirit of Domination

The crucifixion marks the end of the terrible course of temptations that Jesus knew. It marks the end of all the human temptations. These go from the most commonplace to the most flamboyant, heroic, and spectacular. Each time, we saw how Jesus actually overcame whatever derived from human "nature," that which, at the deepest level, is characterized by covetousness and the spirit of power. He overcame *in himself* all covetousness and all will to power. We can also overcome in him . . . because he did. Henceforth, it is a dreadful error to hope to overcome these fundamental powers[23] by ourselves, in our own strength, through mortifications and flagellations and deprivations in order to mortify the flesh.[24]

23. It is important that we do not forget that sexuality is not "in itself." It is not the deepest part of our being nor the most decisive one: sexuality is itself dominated by covetousness on one hand and the Spirit of power on the other. It is only an instrument (among others) of these two powers that are the true frame of the flesh.

24. To mortify . . . is in reality "to make dead." Why not then, go all the way,

For that would immediately lead us into the infernal circle: I am able to overcome my pride through acts of humility—like the publican, I sit down in the last row and immediately pride myself for being so humble—and I give thanks that I am not the Pharisee! Or I flagellate my body to overcome my sexual desire, and then I experience acute pleasure from this flagellation—which becomes for me the substitute for sexual pleasure. . . .

In reality, if Jesus overcame what is the structure of human nature in its autonomy from God, and if—being fully human—he really liberates us from the inevitability of human evil, then, because of this very fact, we can only call on *him alone*. Henceforth, there can never be any "faith in humanity" as we so often hear! No, no faith in humanity is possible. Neither is the theological formulation "God became man so that man might become God"—which is the ultimate demonic temptation for us. No, Jesus became man so that people might become fully human, a real creature, a free creature, freely loving God his creator and savior. Loving and believing by faith and out of such freedom that his obedience is no longer obedience but a simple and happy response to the discovery of this great love—this love by which God so loved the world (that is, each of us) that he identified with us to overcome these temptations in us. No faith in humanity is any longer possible, only faith in the Son of God who became the Son of Man. Only this liberates us and makes us more than conquerors in temptation.

In meditating on the terrible temptations facing Jesus in Gethsemane and on the cross, we have understood that the final temptation harks back to the first temptation at the beginning of his ministry.

Israel and All Peoples

In closing, we have two temptations left to discuss. These are less obvious than all the preceding ones, and they might even surprise

---

and if we have not understood that the question is putting the flesh to death spiritually, let us commit suicide.

some readers. Did Jesus have a clear consciousness about his ministry? He was—and he knew that he was—the Messiah of Israel. But was he also the savior of the world? The contrast between two essential texts manifests this crisis: after choosing the twelve, he immediately sends them on a mission to proclaim the good news. He starts out by saying, "Do not go among the Gentiles or enter any town of the Samaritans. Go rather to the lost sheep of Israel." It is only to the sheep of Israel, the chosen people, that he sends the proclamation that "The Kingdom of God is near!" (Matt 10:5–6). Here, the ministry is very specific and *limited*. After the harsh opposition he meets, he then suddenly enters into the territory of Tyre and Sidon. The text says that "He withdrew" (Matt 15). There is no question of preaching there or performing miracles. He withdraws in the face of the threat from the authorities of Israel and in the face of incomprehension. Anonymous among the Gentiles, he might well be going in search of some rest. This seems to be confirmed by Mark: "He entered a house and did not want anyone to know about it." The Canaanite woman then makes her appearance. When she begs him for help, he does "not answer a word" (Matthew). When she insists, he confirms that he did not come for the Gentiles. He is only the Messiah of Israel. "I was sent only to the lost sheep of Israel." When she continues to insist, he is very harsh with her, saying, "It is not right to take the children's bread and toss it to their dogs." The people of Israel are the children of God. The Gentiles are dogs! Temptation. Should he go beyond his mission as Israel's Messiah? Should he proclaim the Kingdom to all as a universal gospel? Jesus, the Son of God, faces this question; but is it not a temptation from the devil to want to do more than what the Father sent him to do? Is he going to take the responsibility of putting himself—his fear again—above God? We know the breaking point in the story! The woman is certain of what she is asking. She has an unshakable faith, and she lives in her faith in this man in whom she can see truth and the power to overcome demons. She is willing to be called a dog and accepts everything as long as this man to whom she gives her faith responds to that faith. She has the decisive argument: the dogs eat the crumbs that fall from the children's table. The Gentiles will only be given crumbs—so be it, she does not ask to be considered equal to the people of God, whom she recognizes as such: she only asks for crumbs. She knows that one crumb of what God gave in his Son suffices to overcome the demon. So Jesus gives in. He gives in to what was also a temptation. He gives in as he is confronted with humility, with a full faith, with unconditional love. Having recognized all of this, he gives in, which means that at that moment, he decides that he has also been sent to the Gentiles, that the gospel is universal, that the Kingdom of heaven is open to all, and that he is not going beyond the mission given him by the Father. Love and faith have demonstrated that what could at first be experienced as a temptation was not actually a temptation, but instead the human cry to this God who would now be acknowledged as the God of all without exception.

The Fulfillment of the Scriptures

Here is another positive temptation like the preceding one: it is about the fulfillment of the Scriptures. How can generations of Christians have considered themselves freed from the "law" and the "Old Testament" when Jesus scrupulously followed everything that was written there? And not only freed from the ceremonial and moral prescriptions—we have seen how he often breaks those (the Sabbath, washing before meals, purifying oneself after touching a leper or a dead body, and so forth). Each time a transgression of that order appears, it is always to show the deeper, the spiritual, and the true meaning of this same law. What he transgresses against is on the one hand the appearance and on the other that which has been changed, that which has made a spiritual law into a juridical law and made the revelation of freedom into a set of constraints.

On the other hand, he is constantly grappling with untold numbers of prophecies that must be fulfilled because they are prophecies concerning the Messiah! Yet, he does not adhere to them "word for word." He is sovereignly free but fulfills details that take on a huge importance through his life and his death and also fulfills phrases that have only one reason for being—their fulfillment in him. After this fulfillment, they no longer have an exceptional value for us Christians. At the time of his arrest, he asks his followers for swords so that there might be a fulfillment of the words "he was numbered with the transgressors" (Luke 22:37). In order for Scripture to be fulfilled, he must arbitrarily appear to be a bandit or a guerilla fighter . . . On the cross he says, "I thirst" so that Psalm 69 might be fulfilled ("they gave me vinegar for my thirst"). His whole life is punctuated by this fulfillment, yet it was not the *concern* to seek to fulfill. Rather, it is the case that he who is the Word so identified with the Word of God, this word that is so much the Spirit of his spirit that whatever he does, even spontaneously, becomes the living word of what had been proclaimed for more than five centuries. It was recorded so that nothing would be lost of that which could enlighten us as to who Jesus is, nothing relating to this singular being, unique and incomprehensible, Jesus among men. To understand him, it was necessary and *it is still necessary* to go back to this transcendent word, without which the life of Jesus is a riddle that our mediocre ideologies seek to monopolize in order to make themselves important. Here the temptation was: "As the Son of God and as the eternal Word, do I have to obey this progressive revelation, or am I myself the revelation that needs no other?" In all his human depth Jesus obeyed.

The Last Temptation

Just as we have reached the last of his suffering, we now reach the last of his temptations in this great cry: "My God, my God, why have you forsaken me?" Why are the heavens suddenly empty? Why is God so far away that it seems as if he no longer is? Why has the work that you sent me to do ended with this failure? Why this suffering? The temptation that presents itself is the temptation of despair. For this is indeed a cry of despair: if God has abandoned this man, his Son, then nothing more stands and one cannot trust this God who is "mute, blind, and deaf to the cry of creatures." This is the temptation of despair, the ultimate one; no temptation is more terrible—the church was right when it judged suicide, the expression of despair, to be the most serious sin . . . "I know that you are my God, and I declare it; but you are a God who no longer loves me and in whom I can no longer hope." And here, all who may experience despair must know that the Son of Man experienced it before them so that he might be with them and so that even this horrible agony of the soul and of the whole being would not be foreign to God.

Yet, as he undergoes this temptation, the Son of Man declares, "Everything is fulfilled."[25] Now that I have known the worst of what a person can experience, there can be nothing beyond. There can be no temptation that has not been mine, and I have accomplished everything. Suffering and temptation in their entirety are now in God. Whether or not we know it and whether or not we want it, it is so. There can be nothing horrible for people that has not been experienced by this man and taken up by God himself. "Why have you forsaken me?" For, "it was necessary." It was necessary, not to please God, but to carry all of human misery into the heart of God.

25. This is the Louis Segond translation.

BIBLIOGRAPHY

Barbusse, Henri. *Jesus*. Trans. Solon Librescot, with Malcolm Cowley. New York: Macaulay, 1927.

Chouraqui, Andre. *La Bible*. Paris: de Brouwer, 1985.

Communauté de Pomeyrol. *Le chant des bien aimés*. Strasbourg: Oberlin, 1984.

Dreyfus François. *Did Jesus Know He was God?* Trans. Michale Wrenn. Chicago: Franciscan Herald, 1989.

Maillot, Alpfonse. *Les miracles de Jésus*. Paris: Bergers Mages, 1993.

Pernot, Hubert. *Les Quatre évangiles: Nouvellement traduits et annotés*. Ed. Octave Merlier. 2nd rev. ed. Paris: PUF, 1962.

Ruff, Pierre-Jean. "Marie Madeleine." *Evangile et Liberté* (1989) n.p.

Saunders, Cicely. "Hospice, lieu de rencontre pour la Science et la religion." In *Le Savant et la Foi: Des Scientifique S'expriment*, ed. Jacques Arsac et al., 273–76. Paris: Flammarion, 1988.

Thiessen, Gerd. *L'Ombre du Galiléen*. Paris: Cerf, 1988.

Vahanian, Gabriel. *La condition de Dieu*. Paris: Seuil, 1970.